MISSISSIPPI COUNTY COURT RECORDS

from

The May Wilson McBee Papers

CLEARFIELD

Originally published
Greenwood, 1958

Reprinted
Genealogical Publishing Co.
Baltimore, Maryland
1967

Reprinted for
Clearfield Company by
Genealogical Publishing Co.
Baltimore, Maryland
1994, 1999, 2008

Library of Congress Catalogue Card Number 67-29601
ISBN-13: 978-0-8063-0218-8
ISBN-10: 0-8063-0218-6

Made in the United States of America

TABLE OF CONTENTS

PREFACE

These records were not compiled for publication but,
by special request, are made available to those interested.
Hence the informal format. One hopes, however, that they
may be helpful to researchers in genealogy and diverting
to students of the early days of the six counties included.

The legal details of Mrs. Sarah Dorsey's gift of
Beauvoir to Jefferson Davis, as recorded in Harrison County,
ends the collection.

Greenwood, Mississippi

November, 1958   May Wilson McBee

Book A.

p. 68.. April 15, 1806. John and Mary Foster to Jeremiah Bass.

p. 210. Jan. 8, 1810. Archibald Rhea, for love and affection to my children, Andrew, Jesse, John, Wm. Dast, Catherine, Mary, Esther and Betsy.

p. 244. Nov. 12, 1811. Robert Munson, for $3525, to Daniel Clark, of N.O., mortgage on 2200 acres on Buffalo Creek of Wilkinson County, 1600 acres, 1000 acres of which has been previously conveyed by sd Daniel Clark to John Collins, a Spanish grant to Gilbert Leonard. Edw. Randolph, Esq., atty. for Munson. Wit: Robt. Semple, Jno. Bell, R. Davidson. Rec. Nov. 18, 1811. (Adams Co., Miss. Ter. Will of Daniel Clark, of N.O., Aug. 17, 1813-Oct. 1813. Estate to mother, of Germantown, Penna. Exrs: Richard Relf and Beverly Chew. Prob. in New Orleans.)

p. 331. Sept. 4, 1813. Archibald Rea and Martha Rea to Right Munson, all of Wilkinson Co., Miss. Ter., for $1000, tract of 100 French acres on Bayou Sarah, part of tract granted to Andrew Hare. (signed) Archibald Rea, Martha(X)Rea. Wit: Field P. Hunter, Ruffin Deloach, Andrew Rea, Wm. Keary.

p. 365. Dec. 31, 1813. Robert Munson, for $3490 to John H. Johnson, of Parish of Feliciana, La., mortgages nine slaves, names and ages given, 4 horses 74 cattle, two yokes of oxen, one cart, tools, four feather beds, furniture, etc. Wit: Hugh Reid, Thos. Scott.

p. 396. May 12, 1815. I, John H. Johnston, of Parish of Feliciana, La., renounce all my right to the negroes and other property to within named Robert Munson, except the girl Jenny sold to Peter McGraw, and Peter who is dead. Signed. Wit: Joseph Johnson.

p. 416. May 8, 1816. Nancy Ruff, wife of George Ruff, Sarah Yarborough, wife of John F., Lucretia Metz, wife of George Metz, daughters of Delilah Gaines, formerly wife of Richard Strother, dec'd., their father, give power of attorney to Burt May, of Fairfield County, S.C., to secure legacies due them by last will and testament of Jesse Fort. Signed by George Ruff, John F. Yarborough, George Metz. Wit: Washington Lyles, John Dickson.

p. 438. Aug. 19, 1815. Robert Munson, of Wilkinson Co., Miss. Ter., for $1200, to Theney Johnson, of Feliciana Parish, La., negroes, Ellick and Mariah, his wife, and four children. Wit: Jno. Nesmith, Hugh Reid. Rec. July 1, 1816. (Thenia Munson, dau. of Robert, married John Hunter Johnson, son of Isaac and Mary(Routh) Johnson, of Feliciana Parish, Louisiana.)

p. 439. Aug. 19, 1815. Robert Munson, of Wilkinson Co., for $400, to Celia Tuell, three negroes. Rec. July 1, 1816.

p. 440. Aug. 16, 1815. Robert Munson, of Wilkinson Co., for $400, to Telfair Munson, Feliciana Parish, negro Nelso, aged 15. Wit: Jno. Nesmith, Hugh Reid. I do hereby assign to Samuel Tuell the within bill of sale in the full terms of Guarantee made to me by Robt. Munson, for value received, Sept. 4, 1815. Wit: H. Hampton. Recorded July 1, 1816.

p. 440. Aug. 19, 1815. Robert Munson, of Wilkinson Co., for love and affection to my son, Telfair Munson and my two daughters, Celia Tuell and Theny Johnson, all of Feliciana Parish, La., all my stock of horses, cattle and hogs. Wit: Jno. Nesmith, Hugh Reid. Recorded July 1, 1816.

Book B

p. 101. May 13, 1817. Samuel Munson, of Rapides Par., La., to Andrew Rea, for
$2000, 100 acres on Bayou Sarah, part of 1000 acres granted to Andrew Hare, it
being a tract conveyed by Rea and his wife to Right Munson. (signed) Sam Munson.
Wit: Wm. Deloach.

p. 111. April 1, 1818. Issac Johnson to Sarah Dillahunty, both of Wilkinson Co.,
for $100, quit claim to 48 acres on Thompson Creek, adj. Isaac Johnson. Wit: Sam'l.
Stockett, Wm. Johnson. (Note: This is not Isaac Johnson, of Feliciana Parish, La.,
prominent for many years in the Natchez District. Sarah Dillahunty and William
Johnson, in this deed, were children of the above Isaac Johnson and Samuel Stockett
was his son-in-law.)

p. 113. April, 1818. Isaac Johnson, of Wilkinson County, to Joseph Johnson, for $1230,
130 acres. Same witnesses as above.

p. 115. Aug. 27, 1818. Sarah Dillahunty to Joseph Johnson, for $10, quit claim to 100
acres on Thompson's Creek. Same witnesses.

p. 136. Aug. 27, 1818. In consideration of friendship and esteem I have for Mrs. Susan
Chinn, and for $1.00, for her natural life and for no longer, the dwelling house and
plantation whereon she, at present, resides, with the privilege of using said plantation
to any extent proper within the tract purchased by me of John Nugent, not to interfere
with that portion of said land lying contiguous to the plantation where I now reside
and which I may find it necessary to occupy. (signed) Geo Poindexter. Wit: Cato West.

p. 164. -----, 1819. Henry Hampton, of Ascension Parish, La., to son, John Preston
Hampton, of Parish of Arcadia, La., land called "Sligo", sold to Henry Hampton by
Daniel Clark. Wit: Thos. J. Herbert, Benj. S. Collier. Wade Hampton and wife, Mary,
of Feliciana Parish, La., warrant this title and sign.

p. 421. _____ 1817. Jacob Gibson makes bond for $5000 to Wm. Bell, exr, of Jesse
Fort, who left property to daughter, Mary Gibson, wife of Jacob, if Jacob make
proper settlement of agreement. (Jesse Fort, Jacob Ginton and Wm. Burns erected
a cotton gin and gave bond to keep same repaired. Jesse Fort cound it troublesome
and expensive and gave his share to Gibson and Burns.)

Book C.
p. 154. 27 March, 1821. Thomas C. Land, of Wilkinson Co., to Hugh Connell and Moses
Liddell, of same, for $1700, 328 acres and slaves, mortgage. Isaac Dillahunty, wit.
for Thos. C. Land. Mo. L. Bruce for Mary Land.

p. 260. March 22, 1821. Wm. Bracey and Margaret, his wife, of Monticello, Lawrence
Co., Miss., to Chas. Stewart and Edmund McGee, exrs. of estate of Francis Robertson,
dec'd., of Wilkinson Co., for $700, sell and convey 150 acres in Wilkinson Co.
Both sign. Wit. Harvy Cage, F. Blair, Chas Lynch, Jr.

Book D.
p. 174. 3 Dec. 1823. John Yeiser and Eleanor Addison Yeiser, of Wilkinson Co.,
for $1700, to Dr. Benj. F. Young, tract in Wilkinson Co., the same conveyed to
by William and Elizabeth Yerby, to above John. Signed by both. Wit: John M.
Wilson, James A. Fox. Two articles of agreement follow, dated Dec. 16, 1823.

p. 371. April 26, 1820. Rebecca Terry, of Franklin Co., Tennessee, appoints Joseph
Marlow, of St. Francisville (Feliciana Par., La.) to sell lot in Woodville conveyed
to me by Asa and Cynthia Sapp. Wit. A. Campbell, Mavel Emley. Ack. in Tennessee,
March 5, 1825.

Book D.
p.372. March 28,1825. Rebecca Terry to David Holt,by Marlowe, lot in Woodville.

Book E.
p.358. George Poindexter separates from wife,Lydia, daughter of Jesse Carter; offsp·ing A.G.(Albert George) Poindexter withdraws suit in Natchez and admits George has maintained and tried to educate him in every way. Settlement out out of court,Mch.3,1828.

Book F.
p.52. Sept.5,1828. Mary Ann Land,of Wilkinson Co.,Miss.Ter.,for love,etc., to grand-dau., Lucy Ann Ogden,negro girl,Bet. Wit: W.Tigner,Asa Calvet.

p.52. Sept.5,1828. Same to beloved son, John Land, of Wilkinson Co.,negro girl, Peg. Same wit.

p.53. Sept.5,1828. Same to beloved son,James Land,of District of Chester,S.C. negro, Bet, Sr. Same wit.

p.76. Nov.8,1828. Same to beloved daughter,Mary Ogden, of Wilkinson Co., negro girl,Carolina. Wit: W. Tigner,Benj.Newman.

p.86.Sept.5,1828. Same to beloved grandson,Benj.Tidwell, boy, Luther. Wit: W.Tigner, Asa Calvet.

p.87. Sept.5,1828. Same to Beloved Granddaughter,Mary Ann Woodram,of Wilkinson Co.,negro girl,Ann. Same wit.

p.85. Same to beloved grandson,Joshua Tidwell, negro boy,Fortune.Same wit.

p.125. Nov.17,1828. Mary Ann Land,of Wilkinson Co.,for natural love,etc.,to grandson,Benjamin Todwell,of same, negro Tom,on condition that he,Banjamin Tidwell,take said negro boy in full satisfaction of all right,title and interest whatsoever to several slaves now in possession of Jeptha Irwin:and the sa:d Mary Ann Land, as follows: In possession of Jeptha Itwin: Jim, Tom,Carolina,Virginia, Fortune,Bet and Rebecca and there being in possession of Mary Ann Land: Bet, Peg,Amy,Milly and Luther, all of which are descendants of a certain negro, Milly, which formerly belonged to one John Smith, the father of said Mary Ann Land, and a part of said negroes have been in dispute at law between Mary Ann Land and Jeptha Irwin and which suit is agreed to be compromised and dismissed but in case said Bénj.Tidwell shall not take sd negro Tom in full satisfaction, these presents are to be null and void. Wit: W.Tigner,Asa Calvet.

p.127. Mary Ann Land to gr-daughter,Jincy Irwin,wife of Jeptha Irwin, negro slaves,Jim and Virginia, with increase. Nov.17,1828.

p.441. Nov.4,1829. Bythell Haynes, of Wilkinson Co.,for natural love and affection, to my beloved son,Armistead Haynes, four slaves,(named). Wit: Alfred Ratcliffe, Wm.T.Jones.

p.442. Sept.9,1829. Bythell Haynes to beloved son, Francis B.Haynes,four slaves, (named). Wit: Chas.Ratcliffe,John Haynes,Sr.,Wm.T.Jones.

Marriage Bonds
1805 - 1822

Book A.
p.58. James H.Land and Mary Cook. Samuel Dawson,surety. May 1,1819.

p.134. James Richardson and Mary Swezy,Aug.19,1809.

p.135. Thos.Forman and Franky Richardson, Jan.12,1809, married by
        Josiah Gray,J.P.

Book A.
p.134. Jeremiah Thompson and Sarah Jones, Apr. 25, 1808. Married by David Lea, J.P.

p.220. James Gwin and Delilah Lea, Zachariah Lea, surety. Nov. 6, 1806.

p.246. Samuel Harber(Harbour) and Mourning Kenner Dalton, Ewell Dalton, surety,
         May 13, 1809. Married June 1, 1809, by Josias Gray, J.P.

p.250. Francis B. Haynes and Ann Eliza Tomlinson, John Tomlinson surety. All of
         Wilkinson Co. Jan. 23, 1813.

p.277. Thos. C. Land and Mary Laicy, John Ogden surety, Dec. 16, 1807.
         Married by Wm. Jones, J.P., Dec. 19th.

Archibald Thompson and Mary Montgomery, sureties William and Alexander
         Montgomery, Jan. 2, 1809.

p.337. James Richardson and Priscilla Field, surety, Oliver Sluple, Nov. 8, 1813.

p.338. Jesse Richardson and Elizabeth Richardson, Amos Richards surety, Jany. 21, 1813.

                                     1824-1827
p.56. C. B. Haynes and Louisa D. Howard, Bythell Haynes surety. Charles B. Haynes by
         B. Haynes, atty. (n.d.)

p.107. Henry Richardson and Louisa D. Keller, Andrew Higby, surety, April 22, 1825.

p.109. Wm. Richardson and Elizabeth Curtis, John Connell surety, April 22, 1825.

p.113. Samuel Tuell and Ann B. Hughes, Abram M. Scott surety, June 12, 1826.

p.152. Francis Gildart and Judith C. Bailey, Benj. Eccles surety, Dec. 13, 1823.

                                     1828-1839
p.140. Geo. Poindexter, Jr., and Henrietta Baillie, Richard Stewart surety, July 16, 1830.

p.228. John C. Poindexter and Mary E. Poindexter, F. Davis surety, Jan. 24, 1830.

p.343. Baldwin Haynes and Melissa Murphy, John Petherill, surety.

p.285. Wm. Henry Eggleston and Ann S. Poindexter.

p.287. Echols Terry and Rutha Avery.

p.342. James Cole and Elizabeth Saunders.

p.376. Benj. Land and Patience Tidwell.

p.334. Barnabas Pipkin and Elizabeth M. Hannah.

p.146. Wiley W. Richardson and Margaret Reid.

p.343. George L. Poindexter and Virginia Poindexter, F. Davis surety, July 30, 1833.

                              _____

                                      Wills
Book 1.
p.36. Martha Richardson's Will. Jan. 23, 1832. Wilkinson Co. Sons: John G., James B.,
Jared N., W.H., Francis R., and son-in-law, Hiram Singleton. The first three sons and
son-in-law to have one slave, each; W.H. Richardson to have two negroes and their two
children, and Francis R. to have five slaves, cattle, horses and gig and to annually
pay her, (his mother's) brother, Dempsey Gouldin, $80, during the lifetime of Barney,
the last-named negro bequeathed to him. To granddaughters, Martha Gibson, Mary E.
Richardson, Margaret Richardson, youngest daughter of John G., Martha Richardson,
dau. of Francis Richardson, each a slave; to cousin, Folly Richardson, widow of Richard
Richardson, 3 cows and calves and one steer; to free Jack my Spanish filly. Negroes
to remain together under the direction of Francis Richardson until January 1833 and
(cont. next page)

Book 1.

p. 36. (cont.) proceeds of crop raised to go to pay debts. Son, Francis R.
Richardson, sole executor. Wit; Thos. Lyne, Lewis Garrett, Robert White. June 18, 1832.
Codocil: To son, Francis R. Richardson, negro girl purchased since naking will and
he is to pay my son Jared N. Richardson, of West Feliciana Par., La., $225. But if
she died before the probate of this will and codocil, absolved of this payment.
(signed) Martha Richardson. Wit: Robert White, Jared W. Hendrix, Lewis M. Garrett.
Probated Aug. 1832. (See will of Francis Richardson, husband of above Martha. Two
of their sons married daughters of John and Mary (Dalton)Harbour, of Feliciana Par.)

p. 48. Will of Bythell Haynes, Sr., of Wilkinson Co. Eldest son, Armistead, because
of gift deed to him, has had his share and is to have nothing; 2nd son, Francis Bythell
Haynes to have nothing because of gift deed; son, Charles Baldwin Haynes 3 negroes;
son, Thomas Haynes 3 negroes; eldest dau. Andromache Baird 3 negr o4s; son, John Haynes,
3 negroes; son Wm. Haynes 3 negroes; younger daughter Mary A. J. Haynes 3 negroes;
son Bythell Haynes 5 negroes; son Baldwin Haynes two negroes; son Baldwin Haynes
two negroes; son, John Haynes 80 acres on Buffalo Cr.; son William 80 acres; son
Baldwin Haynes 80 acres; three youngest sons, Bythell, William and Baldwin and
younger daughter, Mary, 3 cows and calves each; to sons, Chas. B., Thomas and John,
50 bu of corn; son Bythell 200 bu; the rest of estate to be sold and money divided
among Charles, Thomas, Andromache, John, William, Bythell, Baldwin and Mary,
Youngest sons, Bythell and Baldwin sole exrs. Feb. 1, 1833. Wit:Robt. Germany, Samuel
Murtry, James G. Geraid. Probated Apr. Term, 1833.

p. 256. Will of Wright Munson, of Wilkinson Co., Miss. Feb. 14, 1813. Sick and weak,
to well-beloved son, Samuel Elder, now known as Samuel Munson, whom I claim as
my begotten son and heir, 100 acres of land adjoining Archibald Rea. It is my will
that my present companion, Patsy Ward, shall receive a decent and comfortable
support out of my estate during her single life. Friends, Gerard Brandon, Sr., and Jr.,
exrs. Wit: Dan. Clarke, John Babcocks, G. C. Brandon. Prob. 11 March, 1815.

p. 258. Will of Jesse Fort, of Wilkinson Co., (n. d.) in good health, lands and
personal estate to be sold on credit of 12 months, except slaves. All to be divided
in four lots. One share to Mary, wife of Jacob Gibson, one share to heirs of Delilah
Gaines, decd., one share to Rachel McMorries, wife of Joseph McMorries, one share
to Lydia Bell, wife of Wm. Bell. (In regard to gin seed deed)To heirs of Wm. Burns
and his wife Martha. $15; to heirs of John Jones and 1st wife, Ann, $15. Signed.
Wit: Peter Smith, John Bell, Peter McGraw. Probated March 11, 1815.

p. 95. Will of Jane Reid, of Wilkinson Co., Jan. 7, 1833. Legatees: sister, Margaret D.
Richardson, wife of Wiley W. Richardson, their son, Henry Richardson; sister, Mary
Reid, wife of William James and their son, Robt. R. James; brother, James Reid and
son, Hugh I. Reid; brother William Reid and children, Mary Jane Reid and Alex. H.
Reid. Wit: William Minans, Wiley W. Richardson. Prob. October, 1833.

p. 185. Nuncupative Will of Calvin B. McGoun, 2 Dec. 1837. To brother, Cyrus, $1000
and all my surgical instruments and library, except such books as Mrs. Magoun may
choose to select from it for herself; balance of property to my family; brother and
wife exrs. Proved by William Halsey and Stephenson Waters, at the house of Calvin
Magoun. The Doctor was in full senses but low in health. He told affiants and Dr. Thos.
P. Richardson to bear witness to his nuncupative will. He died 12;30 A. M. 3 Dec. 1837.
(signed) William Halsey, Stephenson Waters. Probated January 1838.

Book 2.

p. 4. Nancy Haynes' Will, Jan. 2, 1842. To my youngest daughter, Sarah Haynes, for love and affection, negro boy, Nathan, son of Olif; to my beloved son, Francis Bythell Haynes, my negro man, Nathan, son of Creta, but he must pay daughters, Elizabeth Gerald, Mourning P. Haynes, Rosa T. Haynes and Sarah Haynes an equal portion of his value as appraised by three disinterested persons. Wit: Bythell Haynes, W. W. Armistead; Charles B. Haynes. Prob. Sept. 14, 1846.

p. 35. Will of Sarah Strother, of Wilkinson Co., Miss. (n. d.). To my sister, Mary Young all my notes and money, household furniture, etc.; to my nephew, Atticus Slaughter, ten negroes (the negroes to have every Sat. and Sun. free from labor.) I wish Atticus to give my brother, John S. Young, as a present from me, if he is alive, (nothing definite stated); $250 to John Young, my nephew, and $250 to Hardy B. Herring, if they are alive. I am now about to leave for Kentucky, May 22, 1848. I write in a hurry but this is my wishes. (signed) Sarah Strother. Probated Oct. 2, 1848. Francis GildartmJudge of Probate.

p. 122. Will of Wm. H. Dillingham, of Wilkinson Co., Miss. June 12, 1855. Woodville. Legatees: My only sister, Eliza P. Dillingham, one-third of my estate; John P. Dillingham and Annie G. Elder, son and daughter of my dec'd brother, Hannibal, one-third of my estate; W. A. P. Dillingham, nephew and niece, Elizabeth B. Dillingham, one-third of my estate; to Adeline, widow of my brother Joseph and Charlotte, widow of my brother, Hannibal, all my rights in estates of their husbands and $500 each. Prob. May 1857

p. 272. Will of James Hill, of Wilkinson Co., written in my own hand relating to certain properties in Mississippi, Louisiana and Tennessee, revoking all other wills, etc., but not any will of disposition of my property outside of these states. To beloved wife, Jane K Hill my Forest Home plantation, also my money, notes, bonds and other claims or securities on hand at Home at my death or on deposit in Bank in N. O. or in the State of Tennessee. It is my plain and expressed intention that this my last shall only operate to pass such property and effects as I may own and of which I may be seized in Miss., Louisiana and Tennessee and that it shall not operate nor be construed to operate in any manner as to the disposition of any property of any kind I may be entitled to elsewhere, nor conflict with any will I may have already made or may hereafter make of property of any kind owned or held by me in States other than the three, Miss., La., and Tenn. Wife, Jane K. Hill, extrx without bond. To sd wife all property mentioned before for her life only and not in fee simple. This is contrary to Mississippi statutes so I make this plain. She is to have full benefit, control and management for life only. After the death of my wife, Jane K. Hill, all to go to my sister, Mary Riley and her two sons, John E. Rilay and Newton Riley in fee simple, on condition that they do not interfer directly or indirectly with any disposition made by me of property whether in this State or elsewhere. If they interfere then they shall forfeit all bequests in their favor. W. M. Green, Epis. Bishop of Diocese of Miss. or his successor to have annually one-thirteenth part of provision I have made for St. Paul's Church, $200 yearly for five years; my wife to pay H. S. VanEaton, atty-at-law $500 as retaining fee and $2000 for funeral expenses, enclosing my grave and erecting a suitable monument. 11 June 1872. Probated Jan. 2, 1873. Petition of Jane K. Hill says that James Hill died December 1872. No bond. (He is buried in Grace Church Cemetery, St. Francisville, La. A beautiful marble shaft marks his grave and some of his wife's relatives are also buried on the large lot.)

Wilkinson County
Wills

Book 2.
p. 283. Will of Robert R. Richardson, of Wilkinson Co., in feeble health. Children:
Frances Ann Newport, wid. of Robert Newport, decd., Arthur W. Richardson, Edward
E. Richardson, Martha M. Richardson, Sarah C. Richardson, Reverdy Richardson, all
personal and real estate, except house and lot in Jackson, East Feliciana Parish,
La. My sons, Preston A. Richardson and Putnam M. Richardson, have had their
share; beloved wife, Mary E. Richardson house and lot in Jackson during life,
then to children: Arthur, Edward, Martha, Sarah and Reverdy. Son, Preston A. and
wife, exrs. No bonds for guardian of children. No accounting to court. Oct. 4, 1873.
Probated Mch. 20, 1874.

Inventories and Accounts

Book 2..
p. ___ . Will of Francis Richardson, of Wilkinson Co., Miss. Estate to beloved wife,
Martha, and children: John G. Richardson, W. A. Richardson, J. N. Richardson, W. H.
Richardson, F. R. Richardson and Susan Singleton. Chas. Stewart, Zach. Goulden
and Edward McGehee, exrs. Nov. 21, p820. Wit: Samuel Wright, Samuel Goodrich,
Wade H. Goulden. Probated Jan. 29, 1821, by Wade H. Goulden and exrs. (Son,
W. H. was Wade H. Richardson. See Probate Minutes, Bk. 2-138.)

p. 117. Will of Moses Hadley, of Wilkinson Co., Miss. Legatees: Wife Ann and
children. Wife, John B. Posey and Samuel Nicholson, exrs. Wit: James A. Luck,
Sarah Luck, Wm. Cason. Aug. 28, 1818.

p. 236. Inventory of Benj. Strother, decd., Dec. 1818. (merchant). Appraisers,
Francis Keller, Isaac Dillahunty.

p. 237. Inventory of Dr. Nathaniel Henchman, Dec. 9, 1819/

p. 329. Henry Richardson, dec'., died intestate in Wilkinson Co. W. A. Richardson
appointed admr., Sept. 22, 1821.

Probate Minutes

Book 1.
p. 18. Apr. 7, 1817. Will of Henry Richardson was brought to court and proved
by oath of Zachariah Goulden and Jared N. Richardson.

p. 19. Oct. 2, 1816. Admr. granted to John H. Johnson on the estate of Robert Munson.
Edward Randolph security on bond for $4,000. Hugh Reid, Peter Presler and Peter
Smith appraisers. Ordered that real estate be sold. Sale notices in Pinckneyville
and Woodville and at the house of Peter Presler

p. 24. Aug. 24, 1822. Cato West appointed admr. of estate of Wm. R. Poindexter.
Bond of $1000, with John Connell and John L. Bruce, sec.

p. 44. Jan. 29, 1832. Will of Peter Randolph. Wit: Wm. H. Eggleston, B. T. Farish.

p. 45. March 11, 1832. Will of Wesley Chambers. Wit: Dick H. Eggleston, Edw. T.
Farish and R. T. Christmas.

p. 55. Last will of Francis Richardson probated by Chas. Stewart, one of exrs.,
proven by W. H. Golden, one of wit. Letters of admr. to Chas. Stewart, with bond
for $100,000, securities Harry Cage and Hugh Connell. David Cooper, Moses
Liddell, Moses Gordon, Hugh Connell and Archibald McGee, commissioners to
divide estate and set apart widow's dower, Jan. 29, 1821.

p. 55. Feb. 26, 1821. Wm. Richardson appointed guardian of Francis Richardson,
with Archibald McGee and Wm. Mathews security.

Wilkinson County
Probate Minutes

Book 2.
p. 138. Feb. 23, 1824. Ordered that an account presented agst the estate of Francis
Richardson, decd., which acct. was presented to the executors in the time required
by law, owing to the misunderstanding of Wade H. Richardson as to the credit of
41 bales of cotton shipped by Francis Richardson, in his life, to Moses Cox, of
Orleans, which from his affidavit and the letter of said Cox was credited Francis
Richardson, instead of to the Wade H. Richardson's firm. The court being satisfied
of the mistake as well as the justice of said amount, order that estate of Francis
Richardson pay to Wade H. Richardson and Fuqua their amount, $2474.30.

Book 3.
p. 30. Sept. 28, 1824. Rev. Barnabas Pipkin, having produced credentials of ordination,
is given certificate to perform rights of matrimony in the State.

p. 30. Sept. 29, 1824. Order. Exrs. of Francis Richardson, decd., to pay acct, of James
B. Richardson, $588.52. (It may be noted that James B. Richardson was not mentioned
in his father's will, as recorded.)

p. 55. March 1, 1825. Letters of admr. granted to Gerard C. Brandon on the estate
Jesse Munson. Bond for $2000, with Wm. L. Brandon security.

p. 137. On motion of Wm. Eccles, ord. that his acct. of $1306.83 against the estate
of Francis Richardson, decd., be paid subject to note given to Francis Richardson
for $1106.54, etc., leaving $140.08. Apr. 27, 1826.

Book 5.
p. 95. Dec. 14, 1837. Elizabeth S. Eggleston and Wm. H. Eggleston granted letters
of admr. on estate of Dick H. Eggleston, decd. Bond $50,000, with Fielding Davis,
Joseph Reddler and James S. Track securities. (West Feliciana Par., La. Harwood
Jones and Rachel Jones, his wife, and John Tabb and Lucy Tabb, his wife and Mary
Jones, of Dallas Co., Ala. appoint Dick Hardaway Eggleston, of Wilkinson County,
atty. to settle our claims to estate of David Crenshaw, decd., late of La., who was,
last year, in the employment of Bartholomew Barrow, near St. Francisville. Sept. 4,
1824. Before James Craig, J. P.   Thomas Craig, J. P.)

p. 96. Jan. 3, 1838, on vacation. On application of Cyrus S. Magoun, ordered a citation
on Mrs. Mary E. Magoun to appear at Jan. Term to contest nuncupative will of her
late husband. // p. 99. Jan. 4, 1838. Cyrus S. Magoun, one of the exrs, named in will
of Calvin B. Magoun, decd., renounced right to serve. Mary E., widow of Calvin B.
McGoun, one of exrs named in the will renounced right to act as exr. of will of
late Calvin B. Magoun and requested court to appoint her brother-in-law, Cyrus S.
Magoun and Wm. H. dillingham to act as admrs. Signed.

p. 95. Dec. 13, 1837. On application of Cyrus S. Magoun, letters of admr. granted
him on est. of C. B. Magoun. Bond, $40,000. Robt. Smith, W. H. Dillingham.
p. 229. Jan. 26, 1840. On application, Mason E. Saunders granted admr. on estate
of Wm. H. Eggleston, decd. Bond, $50,000, Fielding David, John L. Wall, sureties.

p. 238-9. Ord. citation agst Eliz. S. Eggleston and Wm. H. Eggleston be dismissed.
Whereas a partial settlement of estate of Dick H. Eggleston was presented in this
court, since relationship exists between administratrix and the Judge, he being
brother-in-law of intestate, renders it improper, case removed to Adams County.
Feb. 13, 1840. Judge Francis Gildart, Judge of Probate, Feb. 1840.

p. 323. July 5, 1841. Citation to Ann F. Eggleston, wid. of Wm. H. Eggleston, decd.
to show why she should not have her dower allotted and assigned to her in a certain
lot in Woodville.

* * * * * * * * * * *

Book A-1

p.17. On Feb.18,1800,Ebenezer Smith presented a certain deed to be recorded,
which was done,viz: Mississippi Territory,Pickering County. Ebenezer Smith,
of Bayou Pierre, Ter. and Co.afsd., for $1500, received of my two sons,Julius
and Pliny Smith,of same place, do sell to sd Julius and Pliny 500 acres on
South Fork of Bayou Pierre,adj. Daniel Chamber's land on the west, Taber's
Cr. on the east, which land is particularized by the Plat.(signed) Ebenezer
Smith. Feb.15,1800. Wit:John Armstrong,John Villars, Chileab Smith. G.W.
Humphreys,J.P. (The name of Pickering Co.,the upper of the two counties
formed,1799, from the Natchez District, in 1802, was changed to Jefferson.
A few days later, Jefferson County was divided, the northern part becoming
Claiborne County.)

p.65. Daniel Callaghan to John Smith,Esq., of Cole's Creek,Pickering Co., Miss.
Ter., for $450, 300 acres part of 1000 acres, being the same that Peter Walker,
Esq., left, taking 700 acres, being claimed by James Elliott,Junr.,and by his
father sold to Callaghan, under power from the son, recorded in Gemimina's
Office in New Orleans and conveyed to Pedeclau's Office in N.O., Nov.2,1800.
(signed) Dan Callaghan. Wit: Jas. Campbell,John Brooks. Wm. Thomas,J.P.
Bk.A-1,57. In 1788, the Spanish Govt.granted to Jas Elliott,Jr. 1000 arpens
of land on Cole's Creek.

p.104. Frederick Metsco to John Smith. Conveyance registered 3/23/1801.
Frederick Metsco to John Smith,both of Pickering Co., Miss. Ter., for $200, a
plantation granted to sd Metsco by Baron Carondelet in 1793, containing 300
acres on a branch of Cole's Creek,known as Lick branch. Sept. 16,1800.
Frederick (x) Metsco. Wit: Jno. Girault,Wm. Newman. Mordecai Throckmorton,J.P.

p.108. Feb.23,1801. Daniel Chambers, of Pickering Co., Miss.Ter., to Jesse Smith,
of same, for $700,300 acres on south fork of Bayou Pierre in Pickering Co.
(signed) Daniel Chambers. Wit:Ebenezer Smith, Larkin White. Geo.Wilson
Humphreys,J.P.

p.109. Deed,Jesse and Mary Smith to Thomas Marsten Green. Reg.24 Mch.1801.
Dec.24,1800, Jesse Smith and Mary,his wife, of Pickering Co.,Miss. Ter., U.S.
to Thomas Marsten Green,for $500, a tract on north side of the south fork of
Bayou Pierre,being all that tract granted to Jesse Smith by the then Governor
of Louisiana,the Baron Carondelet, dated Aug.3,1793, 240 acres.Wit: Daniel James,
Daniel Chambers. Ack., Jan.20,1801 before Roger Dixon,J.P. Pickering Co.,Miss.Ter.

p.113. Release and quit claim,Wm.Smith to James Elliot,Reg., 25 Mch.1801.
Whereas there appears on the records of Miss.Ter., March 20,1780, a sale made by
Mr.James Elliott during the Spanish Govt., of three tracts of land containing 600 acres
near Cole's Creek, I do declare the sale null and void,having never closed the
bargain nor given any value therefore. Dec.3,1800. (signed) William Smith.
Wit: G.Debuys,John D.DeLany.

p.184. May 21,1817. Geo.Poindexter and wife,Agatha,both of Wilkinson Co.,
Miss. Ter., to John Foster,of Jefferson Co.,a parcel of land granted by the
Spanish Govt.to Wm.Curtis by patent,dated 28 Feb.1795,b.on north by the bluff
adj.the Miss.swamp,northeast by John Strabraker,other sides vacant, 400 arpents.
Wit:E.Turner as to Geo.Poindexter. R.Metcalf,Miss.Ter. Walter Leake,Adams Co.

p.222. 5 March 1818. James Kempe and Francis S.Girault,of Natchez, Miss. to
John Foster,of Jefferson Co., Miss., for $10,000,400 arpents in Jefferson Co.,being
that tract that John Foster and wife,Mary,conveyed to Jas.Kempe and Francis S.
Girault,as above, also an undivided half of 320 arpents in ConCordia, La.,conveyed
to Kempe and Giraultas above, also an undivided half of 320 arpents in county of
Concordia, La. about 7 miles above Natchez, and slaves. Wit:C.Pettibone,Henry
H.Cox. I taylor,Reg.

Book A-2

p. 72. Wm. Moss to Wm. Smith, deed. Registered Feb. 7, 1803. Sept. 8, 1802. Wm. Moss, of Jefferson Co., to William Smith, of Union Town, for $200, sold one house, No. 2, Square No. 19, in Union Town. (signed) Wm. Moss. Wit: J. Stedman, Silas L. Payne. Ack. Nov. 12, 1802. Edward Turner, C. J. C. C.

p. 113. Deed, Wm. Smith to David Phelps, filed July 15, 1803. July 11, 1803, Wm. Smith sells to David Phelps, both of Jefferson Co., Miss. Ter., for $750, lot No. 2, in Sq. No. 19, in Union Town, Jefferson Co., Miss. Ter. Signed. Wit: James Chamberlain, Lewis D. Walker, James Ferguson. July 14, 1803.

p. 235. Deed, Wm. Smith to Rosana Harris, recorded May 7, 1804. William Smith, of Jefferson Co., Miss. Ter., to Miss Rosanna Harris, step-daughter to Adam Snider, a certain bureau which was executed for a debt of Snider's and redeemed by me for $30. March 6, 1804. William Smith. Test: Moses Black, J. Stedman. Before David Phelps, May 5, 1804.

Book B-1.

p. 9. Apr. 17, 1804. Henry D. Downs and Joseph Downs to William Brooks, lot No. 17, 100 sq. poles in town of Greenville. Wit: John Brandt, E. Hospinsed.

p. 14. Deed: John Smith et ux. to John Hopkins. Rec. 2 July 1804. 29 June, 1804, John Smith and Mary, his wife, of Jefferson Co., Miss. Ter., to John Hopkins, of same, for $900, a certain tract, 300 acres, on north fork of Cole's Creek, being part of a tract granted by the Spanish Govt. to James Elliott, Jr., 20 Oct. 1788 and conveyed by James Elliott, as atty. in fact for James Elliott, Jr., to Daniel Callahan and by Callahan by deed to said John Smith, Nov. 21, 1800, bounded by 700 acres of Peter Walker and 241-acre tract granted to Elliott, Sr. John Smith, Mary Smith. Test. Evd. Green, John A. Davidson. John Shaw, J. P. 2 July, 1804.

p. 29. George Winn to Wm. Smith, filed Nov. 23, 1804. Aug. 7, 1803. George Winn, of the City of Natchez, to Wm. Smith, of Jefferson Co., Miss. Ter., for $675, a lot of ground in the town of Union, Jefferson Co., No. 1, Sq. No. 15. (signed) George Winn. Wit: James Wallace, Philip Alston. Bryan Bruin, Territorial Judge.

p. 30. John C. Johnson and John Rail to Wm. Smith, mortgage, filed for record, Nov. 23, 1804. June 6, 1804, John C. Johnson and William Smith, both of Jefferson Co., Miss. Ter., a house and lot lying in Union Town, Lot No. 2, Sq. No. 19, a mortgage. If notes are paid the above is null and void. (signed) John C. Johnson, John Rail. Wit: Edward Hinds, James Metlock, L. Murray. David Phelps, J. P.

p. 38. Mortgage, William Smith to Abijah Hunt. Rec. Dec. 27, 1804. Nov. 23, 1804. William Smith, of Jefferson Co., Miss. Ter., to Abijah Hunt, of same, one house and lot in Town of Union, No. 1, Sq. No. 15, and Lot No. 2, Sq. No. 14, each one-half acre, also slaves, stock, furniture, notes, bonds, crops. If Wm. Smith should pay $1500 with interest before Jany. 1, 1806, the above condition shall cease. Both sign. Wit: Elijah Smith, John Moore, Jo. A. Parrott. John Shaw, J. P.

p. 41. Robert Throckmorton to Abijah Hunt and Elijah Smith, mortgage. Rec'd. 27 Dec. 1804. Oct. 1, 1804. Robert Throckmorton, of Jefferson Co., Miss. Ter., to Abijah Hunt and Elijah Smith, merchants of Natchez, for $375, 600 acres where I now live, one negro fellow, London, one negro woman, Myrtilla, stock, household goods, furniture, etc., unless notes are paid before Jan. 1, 1806. Signed by the three. Wit: John More. Before John Shaw, J. P.

Book B-1

p. 187. Covenant between William Collier, Mary Smith, alias Mary Collier, and
Thomas Calvit, filed 27 June 1807. 27 June 1807, William Collier, of Jefferson
Co., Miss. Ter., and Mary Smith, alias Mary Collier, late widow of John Smith,
decd., now wife of Wm. Collier, and Thomas Calvit, of afsd Co. and Ter.
Whereas the said Mary, at the time of her intermarriage with William was entitled to a considerable estate, real and personal, as well as by force of the
last will and testament of John Smith, dec'd. Whereas differences and disputes
have arisen between William and Mary in consequence of which they have agreed
to live hereafter perpetually separate and apart from each other, each of them
does utterly denounce all right to possession, etc., as husband and wife. Jany. 1st
next, William is to be paid £1250. All the slaves and other personal estate of
Mary which because of their marriage in possession of William, shall be granted
to Thos. Calvit, in trust, Mary to have the rents, issues, profits of the real estate
and slaves during her natural life and upon her death, Calvit shall convey same
to the heirs of John Smith, dec'd., according to his will. William Collier, Mary(x)
Smith, alias Collier, Thomas Calvit. Wit: Seth Lewis, D. W. Brazeale, Wm. Snodgrass,
J. P. Jefferson Co., Miss. Ter., of U. S. June 27, 1807.

p. 271. Deed, Wm. Smith to Abijah Hunt, filed June 14 1808. Sept. 14, 1807. Wm.
Smith, of Claiborne Co., Miss. Ter., to Abijah Hunt, of Natchez, for $625, hath sold
Lot No. 1, Sq. No. 15 in the town of Union in Jefferson Co., containing one-half
acre, it being the lot on which Mrs. Waters now resides. (signed) William Smith.
Wit: Elijah Smith, Moses Liddell, Sept. 23, 1807. Wm. Snodgrass, J. P.

p. 319. Elihu H. Bay to T. and J. Smith, deed of release, filed 30 Mch. 1809.
May 10, 1807, Elihu Hall Bay, of the City of Charleston, South Carolina, by Edward
Turner, Esq., formerly of the town of Washington but now of Greenville, Miss. Ter.,
his attorney, for $304, to Thomas and James Smith, sons and devisees of John Smith,
dec'd., of Jefferson Co., has released and forever quit claimed all that tract of land,
152 acres on the waters of Cole's Cr., mentioned in the original grant of 600 acres
granted by former British Govt. of West Florida to John Smith by patent, dated July 22,
1769 and now by Elihu H. Bay contained in the lines of one or more tracts of land
granted to said John Smith by the Spanish Government May 10, 1807.
(signed) Edw. Turner, atty in fact for Elihu H. Bay. Wit: Thomas West, F. L. Turner.
Wm. Snodgrass, J. P. (John Smith stated that he had come down the Ohio River from
Pa., and found the West Florida lands on the Mississippi River exceedingly good:
that in the spring of 1769 he would bring his wife and family of five. p. 97. Clinton
N. Howard. British Development of West Florida, 1763-69.

p. 363. April 5, 1809. Henry Green and Jane, his wife, of Jefferson Co., Miss. Ter.,
to William Brooks, of Adams Co., Miss. Ter., a tract of land on North Fork of Cole's
Creek, 600 arpents, which land was granted to Henry Green by the Spanish Govt.,
1st Sept. 1795. Wit: Joshua Downs, Jno. Doherty. Filed Sept. 22, 1809.

p. 423. William Brooks et ux to Henry Green, filed Apr. 5, 1809. William Brooks
and Celeste, his wife, of Miss. Ter., Adams County, to Henry Green, of Jefferson
Co., Miss., a parcel of land in town of Greenville, including Lot No. 17, containing
110 sq. poles and another lot, adjoining the public square and lots owned by Geo.
Clare, Wm. Smith and Job Stapleton. Wit: Joshua Downs, J. Doherty, Betsy Towson.
Rec. Sept. 1809.

Book B-1

p. 433. Filed May 18, 1812.   Indenture, May 16, 1812, Asa Searcy and Frances, his
wife, of Jefferson Co., Miss. Ter., to Wm. H. Smith, of same, for $1500, that lot of
land adjoining the north side of the public square in the town of Greenville,
Jefferson Co., including Lot No. 11, with all building, etc. Asa Searcy, Frances(x)
Searcy. Wit: Daniel James, Jacob Wright. Thos. Hinds, J. Q. May 16, 1812.

p. 496. Dec. 1, 1811. Peter Chambliss, of Jefferson Co., Miss. Ter., to Elijah Smith,
of the City of Natchez, three promisory notes, payable Jan. 1, 1813, 1814 and 1815,
for $5924. 26 and for the sum of $1. 00, mortgages tract of land on which I now
live and on which a cotton gin known as the Red Lick Cotton Gin, tract containing
429 acres in afsd Co. and Ter., originally claimed as a preemption by James
Milligan and by him sold to Thomas Fitzpatrick and by him to Peter Chambliss.
Should Chambliss pay said sum the above is null and void.(signed)Peter Chambliss.
Wit: David Hunt, Jas. Cowdon, Jr. Thomas Hinds, Chief Justice, June 1812.

Book C-1

p. 69. Wm. Stampley and wife to D. Hunt and Elijah Smith. Filed Jan. 1, 1814.
Aug. 5, 1813. Wm. Stampley and Patience, his wife, of Jefferson Co., Miss. Ter.,
to Elijah Smith, of Adams Co. and David Hunt, of Jefferson, for certain sums to
them owing, mortgages that tract of land on which Stampley now resides in
Jefferson Co. on the road leading from Greenville to Natchez, adj. lands of Cato
West and Eben Rees, containing 600 acres held by Stampley under a certificate
of donation from the U. S. Commrs. but is to be given to the parties of the second
part if the notes are not paid. Wm. Stampley, Patience (x) Stampley. Wit:Jo Dunbar,
J. Cowden. Rush Nutt, J. Q. Jan. 1, 1814.

Book 1.

p. 154. Sept. 3, 1814/ James Smylie, sole surviving admr. of the estate of Thos. Smith,
late of Jefferson Co., of Amite Co., Miss. Ter., to James C. Wilkins, of Natchez, Miss.
Ter., lands, tenements of John Smith sold at public sale by the admr., 587 acres on
Fairchild's Cr., bounded by Ross, Mark Cole and Bay tracts. Witness: William Yerby.
S. Brooks, Justice of the Quorum.

p. 177. Abraham Scriber and wife to James Smith, deed. Filed July 24, 1815.
Mch. 30, 1815, Abraham Scriber and Jemima, his wife, to James Smith, all of
Jefferson Co., Miss. Ter., for $880,   110 acres in afsd county on waters of Fairchild's
Cr., being part of a tract granted to Parker Carradine by the Spanish Govt. and con-
veyed by his heirs to the late John Smith, of Jefferson County and which fell to
Thomas Lovell and wife, Mariah, by a division of J. Smith's land and conveyed by
Thos. Lovell and Mariah to Abraham Scriber. Abraham Scriber, Jemima(x) Scriber.
Wit: Jas. G. Wood, Alex Young, Justices of the Peace, Mch. 30, 1815.

p. 264. March 19, 1808. Jesse Lum, of the Territory of New Orleans, to Randal
Gibson and William Foster, exrs. of the will of William Lum, conveys a tract of
land granted by the British Govt. to Jesse Lum, Wm. Lum and Hannah Lum, dec'd,
on Cole's Creek near Union Town and bounded by Wm. Ferguson on the south.
Wit:David Gibson, I. Taylor, Miss. Ter. Thomas Rodney, J. P.

Book A

p. 70. John Poor Smith and wife to Elizabeth Green, a deed. John P. Smith, of Rutherford Co., Tenn., to Elizabeth Smith, of Jefferson Co., Miss., all that tract known by the name of Smi h's Bluff Plantation, also a tract adjoining, awarded to John P. Smith, as one of the heirs of John Smith. (signed) John Poor Smith, Frances L. Smith. Wit: James Smith, Wm. Rutherford, Sam'l. K. Sorsby. Rutherford Co., Tenn., Murfreesborough Office. Feb. 22, 1819. Blackman Coleman, Clk. F. Barfield, J. P.

p. 174. John Slater et al to Ann Foster, March 21, 1821. Richard Armstrong and Sarah, his wife, Joseph Slater and Martha, his wife, Samuel Fletcher and Margaret his wife, to Ann Foster, all of Jefferson Co., Miss., their parts of a tract belonging to the estate of Hugh Slater, deceased, on the north fork of Cole's Creek, b. on north by Joel Selman, west by Alexander Phase, south and east vacant, 314 acres.

p. 253. 29 January, 1822. Indenture between William Cook and Jane, his wife, of Claiborne County, and John Dobbs, of Jefferson County. William and Jane, for $350 sell all tract of land on Cole's Creek, Jefferson Co., Miss., containing 23 acres, being a part of a tract entered by Jesse Cook and is the dividend, or share, of said William Cook in the division of landed estate of said Jesse Cook, among his heirs by order of the court, as will belong to him on the decease of Rachel Cook, relict and widow of said Jesse Cook, which the said Rachael now holds in her dower. (signed) William Cook, Jane Cook. Ack. by William Cook Jan. 29, 1822 before Cowles Mead, J. C. C. of Jefferson County. Recorded 28th February, 1823.

p. 320. 23rd June 1823. Whereas by last will of Henry Craig, late of Jefferson Co., dec'd., he required that a tract of land occupied by and through a marriage with his first wife, a daughter of Jesse Cook, dec'd., be sold for the benefit of his children. State Legislature approved 30th June, 1822, authorizing the Orphans Court of Jefferson Co. to order Executor of Craig's estate to sell tract belonging to the heirs of Henry Craig, dec'd., containing 23 acres on the waters of Cole's Creek, bounded by lands of Cowles Mead, Fielding Cook and John Dobbs. Court ordered court to do so, to the highest bidder on 23rd June 1823; Cowles Mead the highest bidder, $200; sold to him. (signed) John Donns, executor. Ack. by signer 5th August 1823, before Isaac N. Selser, J. P. Recorded 1st Dec. 1823.

p. 321. 18 March 1823. Between John Dobbs, Benjamin Williams, Fielding Cook, Tyree Cook and William Cook, of Jefferson County, Miss., of first part and John Dobbs, executor of the last will of Henry Craig, dec'd., of Jefferson Co., in consideration of $1000 doth sell a parcel of land in Jefferson County, on North fork of Coles Creek, 100 acres, bounded by lands of Cowles Mead, John Dobbs, estate of Jonathan Jones and school land, it being a part of a certain tract of land entered by Jesse Cook, of 300 acres and divided by a line to be run by the said Jesse Cook in his lifetime. (signed) John H. Dobbs, Benj. Williams, Fielding(x) Cook, William Cook. Ack. by all July 25, 1823, before Thomas Vaughn, J. Recorded August 5th, 1823.

Book A

P. 350. 2nd June 1824. Between John H. Dobbs, executor of the last will of Henry
Craig, dec'd., and Benj. M. Bullen, all of Jefferson Co., Miss. Whereas agreeably to,
directions of last will of Henry Craig, dec'd., it was directed that a certain tract
of land, containing 100 acres more or less, on waters of Cole's Creek, county afsd,
adj. land of Cowles Mead; the heirs of Jesse Cook, dec'd. and by a reserved section.
Now this indenture witnesseth that party of first part, by virtue of said will and consideration of $896.00 has sold tract lying in aforesaid County on Coles Creek,
100 acres, more or less, (except 23 acres heretofore sold by executor of last will of
Henry Craig to Cowles Mead, 23 June 1823), bounded on North by lands of heirs of
JesseCook, dec'd.; South by lands of Cowles Mead, and is part of a tract of 300
acres patented by the United States to Jesse Cook, now dec'd. and is the south part
of said 300 acres. John H. Dobbs. Ack. by signed 4 June 1824 before A. Johnson.
    Recorded 8th June 1824.

Book B.

p. 107. Walter Strother and wife, Harriet, to Hugh Mathews, 28 July, 1827, for $200,
71 acres, the same allotted to Mrs. Deborah Hartley as her portion, as heir of her
father, John Hartley, which said lot descended to the granddaughter of said Deborah,
Mary Ann Hartley and at her death, without issue, to said Harriet.

p. 208. 13 December, 1821. Pharoby Coleman, Ann Weeks, Dan'l. Greenleaf and
Eunice Lenard of Adams County and Israel Coleman, Elizabeth Coleman, W. Griffing,
Wm. Scott, Ann Scott, Zachariah B. Jones, Elizabeth Jones and Phebe Craig, of Jefferson
Co., all of the State of Miss., for the sum of one dollar, give, sell and quit claim
to John Jones a certain tract of land in Jefferson Co., it being the east end of one
half of tract that did belong to the late Jno. Jones, dec'd. and was by him willed to
his son John. (signed)Pharobah Coleman, Israel Coleman, Elizabeth Coleman, W.
Griffing, William Scott, Ann Scott, Zachariah E. Jones, Elizabeth Jones, Phebe Craig.
Ack. by Pharibah Coleman, Israel Coleman, Elizabeth Coleman, W. Griffing, William
Scott, Ann Scott, Zachariah B. Jones, Elizabeth Jones, 13 Dec. 1821. Ack. by Phebe
Craig 26th Dec. 1821, and by Sarah Griffing and Ann Scott 26 Dec. 1821. Rec.
15 Oct. 1828.

p. 230. Feb. 2, 1824. Bond of Willis Bartholomew and Elizabeth Bartholomew as
guardians of the minor children of David Stampley, dec'd. Securities: Samuel
Dougherty, Samuel Goodwin. Children: Delanson Stampley, David Stampley, Susan
Stampley and the infant daughter, Ursula Ann. (Ursula Ann Stampley married
Abijah Hunt Mundell, the son of Andrew and Polly(Smith)Mundell, of Claiborne
Co., Miss. Andrew Mundell had first married Francesm the sister of Stephen Minor,
of Natchez, and Polly Smith, dau. of David Smith, had married Vachel Dillingham, Jr.
of Kentucky, who died in 1803.)

Book E.

p. 347. April 14, 1842. Moses Foster, of Copiah Co., Miss., and J. L. Tucker, of
Madison Co., Miss., appoint Milford Hunter, of Claiborne Co., Miss., attorney to
sell by private sale all our interest to our undivided shares in the landed estate
of the late Everet H. Jouet, of Jefferson Co., Miss. Jas. S. Johnston, J. P. (Milford
Hunter came to Claiborne Co. from Cape Girardeau Co., Missouri, and became
a prominent lawyer in Mississippi.)

Book D.

p.105. Last will and Testament of John Smith of the Bluff near the place sometime called Villa Gayoyo, in the County of Jefferson and Mississippi Territory.

Item. To beloved wife, Mary, 400 acres of land on which I now live, to include the dwelling house, out houses, gin and other improvements (etc.) and all the negroes and other personal estate of which I may die possessed and which is not herein bequeathed, to have during the term of her natural life, except one-half of said tract in case my son, John Poor Smith shall attain the age of 21 years during her life. It is also my will that my said wife should give each of my children, except Polly Brooks, an equal proportion of beds and furniture, my said daughter, Polly Brooks, has already been proffered.

Item. To my son, John Poor Smith, one-half of 400 acres when he reaches the age of 21 years, or be married and the remainder of the said 400 acres after his mother's death; also 5 negroes (all male) named.

Item. To my two daughters, Anna Maria and Roxana, 300 acres on Lick Branch to be equally divided between them.

Item. I give and devise all the rest of my real estate to my sons, William Smith, Thomas Smith and James Smith to be equally divided between them.

Item. I give to my son William, slaves, (seven in all and named).

Item. I give to my son, Thomas, slaves (Six of them and named).

Item. I give to my son, James, slaves (named five.)

Item, I give to my dau., Anna Maria, slaves (named, five)

Item, I give to my daughter, Roxana, slaves (named five)

Item, I give to each of my children, except my son William and my dau. Polly, 4 horses, 10 cows and calves, one yoke of oxen and ten head of sheep to be in shares as nearly equal in value as possible.

Item. I give my son William 10 cows and calves, one yoke of oxen and ten head of sheep.

Item. I give my daughter Polly Brooks, 10 head of sheep.

Item. I give to wife and children, William, Thomas, James and John, Anna Maria, and Roxana all the proceeds of the crop on the land or unsold at my decease and all ready money which I may have or may be received from those indebted to me, after first deducting my just debts and funeral charges, to be equally divided between my wife and children.

Item. It is my will that my wife, Mary, shall have the use of the estates and other property devised to my children, James, John, Anna Maria and Roxana until the boys arrive at the age of twenty years and the girls eighteen or until they are severally married when they shall be put in possession of their bequests; and in consideration of such use it is my will that my wife maintain and educate my said children.

Item. I give and bequeath all the property herein bequeathed to my wife or not otherwise disposed of and the increase thereof after my wife's death to my children equally, share and share alike. I appoint my wife, Mary, and my sons, William Smith and Thomas Smith executors of this my last will and testament and guardians of my four youngest children. Sept. 27, 1803. Signed. Wit:Rauleigh Hogans, David Davis, William Murray.

Orphans Court Minutes, 1804-1814. Page 17. May 11, 1804. John Smith's will was ordered to be recorded by the Court. Page 59. Thos. Smith and Armstrong Ellis were granted letters of Admr. on estate of Mary Smith, deceased, alias Collier, April 25, 1808. Page 44. June 24, 1807. James Smylie was granted a license as an ordained Preacher, to perform marriage ceremonies.

Book A.

p. 43. Will of Henry Craig, of Jefferson County, State of Mississippi. Dated 26 July
1820, Proved (date not given). I, Henry Craig, weak in body, do make this my last
will, etc. First, I give and bequeath to my beloved wife, Phoebe Craig, all that
part of the estate of Jonathan Jones, being one-third part of same, (as expressed
in last will of said Jonathan Jones, deceased), which I inherited by my said wife
and whereas it would be attended with great inconvenience to separate stock,
consisting of horses, cattle, hogs and sheep, which belonged to said estate, I
therefore give to my wife and her heirs one half of all my possessions in full
of stock received by my wife when we married; to my wife, farming utensils, household and Kitchen furniture, four feather beds and furniture to them belonging,
(one cupboard excepted) all crop of corn now growing. It is my wish, etc. that
the tract of land I formerly lived on, also 23 acres adjoining aforesaid tract and
Col. Cowles Meade, be sold, all balance of stock be sold and money therefrom be
equally divided among my four children, to wit: Rachel Craig, Fenton N. Craig,
Eliza Craig and William H. Craig, except $100.00 to my aforesaid son, William
H. Craig, and $50.00 to my daughter, Eliza Craig. Negroes to be hired out until
youngest child becomes of age, then negroes with natural increase together with
money from their hire and the tract I own in Claiborne County, 320 acres, be
equally divided among my four children, beforementioned. From cotton crop now
growing, I wish all just debts be paid and balance after my funeral expenses I
bequeath one-half to my beloved wife; the other half to be divided among my
four children. Rest of estate to be divided among four children, each to have
share when they become of age, and I do appoint John Dobbs, sole executor.
Signed. Henry Craig. Wit: Thomas V. Vaughan, Charles H. Jourdan and Levi C.
Harris. (His daughter Eliza Craig, married John S. Fulgham, of Copiah County.
Her mother, her father's first wife, was Elizabeth Cook, daughter of Jesse Cook
and his first wife, Rachel.)

p. 107. 11 June, 1829. This is my last will and testament, I being in sound mind
and wishing to settle my worldly affairs, 1st. I give my soul to God. 2nd, it is my
will and desire that all my just debts shall be paid. 3rd. It is my will and desire
that fifty dollars be set apart to be appropriated for enclosing my grave and
twenty dollars be set apart for Christ's Church for its completion. 4th. For my
natural love and affection and consanguinity to Martha Ann Foster, I give and
bequeath my negro boy, Claibourn. 5th. I give and bequeath to my niece, Helen
Jane Foster, my negro woman, Carolina. 6th: I give and bequeath to my niece,
Mary Eliza Foster, my negro girl Peggy and negro child, Susan, dau. of my negro
girl, Lucinda. 7th: I give and bequeath to my nephew, James David Foster, my
negro woman, Lucinda. 9th. I give and bequeath to my friend, Jas. S. Clack,
eight linen shirts and a camlet cloak. 8th: I give and bequeath to Mrs. Mary
Foster, wife of Mr. John Foster, my black horse. 9(sic) I give and desire as my
brother-in-law, John Foster, has assumed the payment of a considerable sum of
money for me, say $12,000, more or less, that he have controul of my affairs and
the property remain in his possession until the hire amounts to full discharge
of all my just debts. 10th. And lastly I do appoint my brother-in-law, John Foster,
my sole executor. In Testimony I have set my hand this day and year above written.
George Brooks. Witness: James Payne, John Foster.

Probate Records. Sec. A. No. 104. John P. Smith, ward. Joseph Dunbar, guardian.
Jefferson County, Miss. Territory. Bond of Joseph Dunbar as guardian of John P.
Smith, infant orphan of John Smith, deceased, bond for $8,000, signed by him
and Isaac Noble. May 16, 1812. Wm. Parker, Reg.

A schedule of the property both real and personal belonging to John Poor Smith,
infant orphan of John Smitj, dec'd. Viz: Tract of land known as Bluff Plantation,
400 acres, 11 negro slaves, one undivided half of 6 horses, 40 hogs, 36 sheep and
7 oxen, other stock, farming implements, household furnishings. Two notes of
Thomas Smith, one for $83.33, dated Feb. 29, 1809; one for $55.00, dated June 27,
1812. Caleb Hill, J. P.

Sec. A. No. 104, (cont) List of vouchers, (17 in all). That of John Snodgrass sold
books such as Murray's Grammar, Immortal Mentor, American Preceptor, Spelling
Book and Arithmetic. E. Shackleford sold shoes for the negroes and for John Poor
Smith. Robert Dunbar sold homespun for two coats and pantaloons and for making
them; board and lodging furnished John P. Smith from April 11 to Oct. 11, 1813,
$36. James Hackett received tuition for John P. Smith at $2.00 per month, for
six months. $1.00 deducted for loss of time. Feb. 3, 1813, Natchez. Parke Walton,
Treas. of Jefferson College received $6 for one quarter's tuition at the College,
Feb. 1, 1813. James Smylie, O. D. M. received $28 for board and tuition. To
Joseph Dunbar, guardian, for "cash" furnished for expenses in travelling to Amite
County. Oct. 24, 1814, service as guardian $15. Final settlement, Oct. 23, 1815.
(This last date was supposed to be when John P. Smith became twenty, so he was
  born in 1794.)

Minutes of the Orphans Court.
  p. 22. Friday, Aug. 28, 1805/ The last will and testament of John Burney, dec'd.
was presented in open court for probate, but delayed, there being neither of the
witnesses present. Only one of the legatees.

  p. 27. On application of Richard D. Burney and John Dennis, ordered that Letters
of Administration be granted them on Estate of John Burney; then sworn; entered
bond with James Bedsel and Asa Searcy securities, sum of $4,000.00 as by law.

  pp. 117, 118, 119, 121, 122. Feb. 1, 1811. Jesse Cook died intestate. Rachel Cook
and John Atkinson apply for Letters of Administration, 4th Monday in January,
1811. Granted. (Rachael was Jesse Cook's widow and John Atkinson her son by
a former marriage.)

  p. 21. Wednesday, Aug. 21, 1805. The last will and testament of Mordecai
Throckmorton, deb'd., was proven in open court by the oath of James S. Rollins
and ordered to be recorded. p. 25. Nov. 11, 1805. John Gerault, the executor
named in the last will of Mordecai Throckmorton, dec'd., came into Court,
took the oath of Executor, etc.

File A. No. 38.
Estate of Edmund Blanton, Sarah Blanton, admx. Appraisal of property of property
of Edmund Blanton, decd., as shown by Sarah Blanton, admx.
1 Rifle gun and shot bag.... $20.00
1 Rifle gun and shot bag with brass mountings ... $18.00
2 feather beds with all their furniture... $50.00
1 bureau...... $30.00
1 breakfast table $5.00
1 trunk $1.50
(continued)

File A. No. 38 (cont.)
1 tea tray, 6 drinking glasses, 4 teacups and 5 saucers, tea pot, tea canister, salts
and pepper box, 6 silver tea spoons and 1 small waiter. $9.00
1 old case and 6 bottle ... $1.50
2 old smoothing irons...... $1.00
1 candlestick and snuffer .. $1.75
6 puter(pewter) spoons...... .37
10 plates and a small dish $2.00
6 chairs $2.25
1 man's saddle $18.00
1 old Bible and Geography...... 25
3 ditto axes...... .... $3.00
1pr old chains and harness... $1.50
3 planes, etc.
Negroes: Tena, Eliza, Denny, Mo, Beckah, Isbell, Andrew, Bob, one woman and six
children Alexander. A tract of land, 48 acres. Total $5363.62. Nov. 22, 1808.
Philip Alston, Collin Nutt, Jas. Droomgoole, appointed by Orphans Court to make
appraisal. Personally appeared Sarah Blanton, admx. of estate of Edmund Blanton,
dec'd., declaring this is original appraisal as returned to by appraisers, Jan. 17,
1809. Thomas Fitzpatrick, J. P.

Return of sale of part of estate of Edmund Blanton, dec'd., Mch. 8, 1809. Total
$265.50. (signed) Sally Blanton.

Citation dated 3rd Feb. 1823 to Sarah Blanton that she appear to settle final acct.
of estate of Edmond Blanton, dec'd. Administration Bond of Sarah Blanton, admx.
of estate of Edmund Blanton signed by Sally Bond, Charles L. Lee, Thomas Fitzpatrick. Finally settled 1823.

We, the undersigned heirs and representatives of John Blanton, do hereby release,
discharge and acquit Sarah Blanton of any claim which we may have had on the
estate of Edmond Blanton, dec'd., hereby avknowledging to have received all that
we may have been entitled to in law and equity. 1ct Jany. 1824. (signed) W. W. Blanton,
Jno. Turnbull for himself and Martha W. Turnbull, his wife, James Berthe, for himself
and Charlotte M. Berthe, his wife, J. L. Martin for himself and H. B. Martin. In presence
of Andrew Turnbull.

File No. A. 333. February Term, 1828. Orphans Court.
Papers in Sarah Blanton's estate. W. W. Blanton, admr., has complied with order
by court to sell undivided interest of the heirs of Sidney Davidson, decd., to
personal estate of sd Sarah Blanton. Nov. Term. 1826.

Book A.

p. 45. William Collier to Mary Smith, 22 Apr. 1807. Thos. Hinds sec.
Wit: Joshua Downs. Married by Thos. Hinds, J. P.

p. 78. Thomas Marble to Elizabeth Jones

p. 79. Prosper King to Susannah Cole

p. 88. John Terry to Sebal O' Neal, 3rd Feb. 1809.
By Christopher Murray.

p. 97. Isaac A. B. Ross to Martha Thomas

p. 130. William Terry to Miss Martha Ker, 28 Feb. 1818.
Married by Adam Cloud, March 1, 1818.

p. 134. David King to Sarah Anderson

p. 153. William B. Prince to Sally P. Jeffers, 9 Dec. 1819.
by Randall Gibson, M. G.

p. 190. I. I. W, Ross to Jane B. Wade, Feb. 1823.

p. 266. P. Montgomery to Marie Davidson.

p. 132. P. Montgomery to Marie Davidson.

p. 132. Abner Wilkinson and Cibel Smith, Aug. 15, 1801
by G. W. Humphreys, J. P.

p. 132. Stephen Terry and Phoeby Smith, Aug. 15, 1801,
by G. W. Humphreys, J. P.

   The date of the last two marriage records and the name of the J. P.
who performed the ceremony show that it took place in what became a
year later Claiborne County but was then the upper part of Pickering
County, as Jefferson was the lower section of it.

Book A.

p. 2.   March 31. 1802. William C. C. Claiborne, Governor of the Mississippi Territory:
To all who shall see these presents: Greetings.   Know ye that I have constituted
and appointed, and by these presents do constitute and appoint William Downs,
George W. Humphreys, James Stanfield, Ebenezer Smith and Daniel Burnett, Esquires,
to be Justices of the Peace and Justices of the County Court for the County of
Claiborne, to hold office with the profits and emoluments thereunto belonging
during the pleasure of the Governor, for the term beginning and do hereby
authorize and empower them to do and perform all and whatsoever to the said
offices and duties of Justices of the Peace and Justices of the County Court
for the County of Claiborne aforesaid, doth anyways appertain and belong.
   In testimony whereof, I have caused the seal of the sd Territory to be
hereunto affixed. Witness: William C. C. Claiborne, Governor and Commander
in Chief, The thirtieth day of January, A. D., one thousand eight hundred and
two and in the twenty-sixth year of the U. S. of America,

p. 3. March 31, 1802. Appointment of James Harman as Justice of Peace, etc.
as above. Signed Governor Claiborne.

p. 4. June 1, 1802. William Smith and Ann, his wife, to David Smith, son of said
William and Ann, for $1000, 300 acres on the Mississippi River, about one mile
south of Bayou Pierre, bounded by lands granted to William Smith by the Spanish
Govt., 5 March, 1789, containing 400 acres, by another 800 acres gr. by Spanish
Govt., 26 Dec. 1895, on the east by lands of Judge Bruin and on the north by
remaining part of the 400 acres, being the same on which sd William now
resides. Wit: Geo. Cochran, Wm. Scott, Arthur Carney. (signed) William Smith.
Ann(x)Smith. Ack. by Wm. Smith, June 1, 1802 in court. (The first registered
deed in the county.)

p. 11. 5 Oct. 1801. Jesse Smith, of Pickering Co., Miss. Ter., and Mary, his wife,
to Abijah Hunt, of Adams Co., gr. to Daniel Chambers by Carondelet, 1793.
Signed: Jesse Smith. Mary(x)Smith. Wit: Daniel Burnett, Henry Hunt, John Gibson.

p. 27. Dec. 13, 1802. The following letter from Joseph Darlington was ordered
by the court to be recorded. Chillicothe, 26 Nov. 1803. Dear Sir: Have wrote
you several times on the subject of the land I purchased in your country.....
my bargain was with your father that if I did not return he was to keep the
land and pay for it. I do not wish to make anything by it for it will cost me
more to attend in person than the difference would be worth... Under the idea
that you will take it yourself I have empowered Col. Bruin to sell and convey
the land as it would be difficult to convey it to yourself had I sent the power
in your name if you should think it proper to become the owner. Please present
my kind wishes to Mrs. Humphreys, Senr., and your Lady and believe that I am
Your humble servant. J. Darlington. To George W. Humphreys, Esq.

p. 28. 13 Dec. 1802. George W. Humphreys, of Claiborne Co. Gives quit claim to
James Davenport on 280 acres, the tract on which William Thompson now resides.
Signed. No witnesses. Ack. same day, in Ct. by G. W. Humphreys before Daniel
Burnett and recorded.

p. 29. Power of attorney. Joseph Darlington, of Ross Co., Ter. of the U. S. North-
west of the Ohio, to Judge Peter Bruin, of Miss. Territory, to convey by legal
title a survey of land, 500 acres, 1789, on James Creek, a branch of Bayou
Pierre. Ross County, Ter. of U. S. Northwest of Ohio. Thos. Worthington and
Samuel Finley, Justices, receive acknowledgement of Joseph Darlington at
Chillicothe, 26 Nov. 1800.

Book A.

p. 30. 25 Sept. 1801. Judge Peter Bruin conveys above land to G. W. Humphreys.

p. 47. 11 Sept. 1802. Julius Smith and Pliny Smith, both of Claiborne Co.,
planters, to Abijah Hunt, merehant. Whereas sd Julius Smith, Jesse Smith, Pliny
Smith and Amos Hubbard, by virtue of several instruments, were obligated, 15 Feb.
1802, for $1000 to said Abijah Hunt, etc., sd Julius and Pliny mortgage to sd
Hunt a tract on the South Fork of Bayou Pierre which was granted by the Spanish
Govt. to Ebenezer Smith, 15 Feb. 1788, and by him deeded to Julius and Pliny,
15 Feb. 1800. If sd Julius, Pliny, Ebenezer and Amos Hubbard pay to sd Abijah
Hunt the above amount with interest, this mortgage is null and void. Signed
by Pliny and Julius Smith. Wit: John Brookes. Recorded 12 Aug. 1808.

p. 122. 31 Dec. 1827. Martin Price, Phoebe Price, his wife, Ralph Price and
Clarissa, his wife,, to Llewellen Price, father of sd Martin and Ralph, for love
and affection, and for the support of said Llewellen 215 acres ...(this deed was
completed on page 288) signed by Martin, Ralph and Clarissa. Wit: Alexander
Montgomery, James W. Smith., ... 1828. Sam'l. Holt, J. P.)

p. 435. May 16, 1829. Thos. Simmons to Jeremiah Thompson, for $300, 80 acres,
21T13-2E. Ack. in court. S. Holt, J. P.

  Book B.

p. 1. Nov. 9, 1805. G. W. Humphreys, of Claiborne Co., to Abijah Hunt, of the City
of Natchez, Miss. Ter., one-half of tract of 1000 acres on North Fork of Bayou
Pierre, called Grindstone Ford, granted to Daniel Burnet by the Spanish Govt.,
1st Aug. 1791 and conveyed to G. W. Humphreys, 27 June 1796. Signed G. W.
Humphreys and Sarah Humphreys. Israel Loring.

p. 102. Nov. 15, 1802. Received by William Smith of Isaac Rapalje, $536, in full
payment of a negro wench, sold to him by the estate of William Moore, dec'd.
(signed) William Smith, admr. Wit: Thos. Gibson. Proved same day in Court by
Thos. Gibson.

p. 119. Feb. 17, 1806. Gibson Clarke, Senr., and wife, Susannah, of Claiborne Co.,
Miss. Ter., to Elias Barnes, of same, for $5000, 600 arpens on fork of Bayou Pierre
and Clarke's Cr., on which he now lives, being a grant from the Sp. Govt. Gibson
and Susannah signed with their marks. Wit: Sam'l. Bridgers, Stephen B. Minor, Elipt.
Frazer. (The above grant was confirmed by the Commrs., 3 June 1805.) Proved
in Court, 24 Jany. 1807, by Eliphalet Frazer, before J. Moore, J. P.

p. 148. 16 March, 1807. Francis Nailer and Maria, of Adams Co., Miss. Ter., to
Elias Barnes, of Claiborne Co., for $1000, a tract on Tabor's Cr., on South Fork
of Bayou Pierre, gr. to James Lobdell, 6 April 1790. Both signed.

p. 161. 22 Dec. 1807. Peter Bryan Bruin to Lewis Evans and George Overaker, tract
adjoining Wm. Smith and George Humphreys. Wit: My. Loring, Abijah Hunt.

p 334. 25 Oct. 1803. These are to certify that Zaccheus Tharp does relinquish
his improvement in the Spanish Country on the south side of Joseph Lake unto
David Christian. Signed: Zacheus Tharp. // 31 Aug. 1804. I do assign the within
to Ezra McCall. Signed: David Christian. Claiborne Co., Miss. Ter., Personally
appeared Eleazer Tharp and made oath that he saw Zacheus Tharp execute the
within instrument and deliver same to David Christian. He, himself, was a witness,
2 Mch. 1809. Signed. G. W. Humphreys, J. P. Rec'd for record, 3 Mch. 1809. John
Patterson, Clerk.

Book C.

p. 90. 13 Dec. 1809. Abel Eastman to William Daniel, both of Claiborne Co.,
for $1000, 200 acres whereon sd Eastman now lives, beg. on upper corner of
Gun's Bayou. Signed by Abel Eastman and Salome Eastman. Wit: Jas. Scarlett,
John Liddy. Ack. in Court, 3 Feb. 1810 before Dan'l. Burnet. (From minutes of
the Court, 1813, " In place of Abel Eastman, dec'd. James Hamilton apptd. overseer of road.) James Hamilton was also an appraiser of estate of Abel Eastman.

p 94. Richard Davidson, of Port Gibson, Claiborne Co., Miss. Ter., of the U.S.,
for $900 paid him by John Cummins, of county afsd., grants etc. the south half
of Lot One, Square 10, in the Plat of the Town of Port Gibson, 16 March, 1810.
Signed: Rich'd. Davidson. Wit: William Lewis, Samuel Frye. Ack. by Frye, 19th
March, 1810, before Thos. Barnes, J.Q. Recorded 18 March 1810 by Jno. Patterson, Clk.

pp. 108-109. Land Grant No. 194. Land Office West of Pearl River, Jany. 1807.
William Smith, of Claiborne Co., on 24 Dec. 1806, entered with the Register of
the Land Office, West of Pearl River, a certificate from the Board of Commrs.
stating that he was entitled by pre-emption to 499-55/100 acres on the waters
of the Big Black at two dollars per acre, for said tract, amounting to $999.10.
He paid $249, 78, one-fourth of purchase price. Signed: Thos. H. Williams, Register
of the Land Office. // p. 109. 16 March, 1808, for consideration of $2500, we
assign the within certificate to Will Lindsay, etc. Signed, William Smith,
Sillitha (x) Smith. Wit: Eden Brashears, Nathan Smith. Proved by oath of Eden
Brashears, a witness, before me, one of the Justices of the Peace and Quorum of
sd County, 9th March, 1809. Signed, G. W. Humphreys. Recorded same day. (The
above is not the William Smith in the following deed. M.W. McB.)

p. 138. (Date missing) William Smith, of Claiborne Co., for natural love and
affection which I bear unto my son-in-law, James Corbet, 57 acres, English
plantation measure, bounded on the north by David Christian, on east by lands
claimed by Lewis Evans and George Overaker, Esqs. and on all other sides by
myself. Signed: William Smith. Wit: James Pryor, Edmond Brewin (Bruin). Feb. 7,
1807, ack. by Wm. Smith before P. B. Bruin. Surveyed Oct. 12, 1808 by Arch'd. Searcy

p. 144. 15 Apr. 1809. Stephen B. Minor to Benjamin Shields, both of Claiborne Co.,
for $400, 230 acres on the south side of Bayou Pierre, being part of 1000 acres
gr. to William Brocus, Senr., dec'd., whereon said Minor now lives. Signed. Ack. by
Stephen B. Minor before W. H. Woolridge, J. P., 23 Nov. 1809. Rec. Nov. 24, 1809.

p. 178. 30 July, 1810. William Smith and Nancy, his wife, of Claiborne County,
to John Smith, to John Smith, son of said William and Nancy, tract, bounded on
south by David Smith; on north by land claimed by James Corbet, on east and west
by Evans and Overaker; for $1010. Signed: William Smith. Nancy(x) Smith. Ack in Ct.

p. 266. 8 Mch. 1810. Andrew Mundell to Israel Loring, both of Claiborne Co., for
$700, as Mundell's interest in 185 acres on North Fork of Bayou Pierre, but he does
not warrant the title to same. Signed. Wit: J. G. Clarke, A. B. Bradford. Agreement
attached: Agreement and lease of land, formerly claimed by Andrew Mandell and
sold to Israel Loring, the same being the land whereon the said Mundell now lives.
The sd Mundell to lease tract from sd Loring and pay him 2000 pounds of seed
cotton for rent and give him possession the 1st of January next. Both signed.

p. 233. 3rd Nov. 1810. Major John Minor, of Concordia, Orleans Territory, to
Allen Barnes, of Claiborne Co., Miss. Ter., for $1600, 400 arpens on the south side
of the North Fork of Bayou Pierre, granted to sd John Minor by Spanish Govt.,
8 June, 1792, and surveyed 6 Jany. 1790. Signed. Wit: S. B. Minor, S. Bullock.
Proved by Stephen Bullock before Thos. Barnes, 4 Nov. 1810. Rec. 7 Nov. 1810.

Book D.

p.3. 8 May Robert Cochran and John Murdock, of Claiborne Co., Miss. Ter.,
to David Christian, of same, for $300, paid, 269 acres on James Creek, (metes).
Signed by both Cochran and Murdock. Wit: Henry Cassiday, Edmonds Bruin. //
Bruinsburg, 22 Dec. 1807. Came Edmonds Bruin before me as witness to above.
(signed) P. Bryan Bruin.

p. 23. May 13, 1811. Stephen B. Minor and Ann, his wife, of Claiborne Co., Miss.
Ter., to Eliphalet Frazer, of same, for $1200, 400 arpents on South Fork of Bayou
Pierre, in sd Co. and Ter., bounded by William Brocus on one side and on the other
by lands of Thomas Creighton, being a grant from the Sp. Govt. by Carondelet,
28 Feb. 1795, and confirmed by U. S. Commrs. West of Pearl River, 4 June 1805,
having been surveyed by Trudeau, 3 Jany. 1794. Signed Stephen B. Minor, Ann Minor.
Wit: J. Moore, John Smith. Ack by Ann Minor before Daniel Burnet, J. Q. 13 Mch. 1812.
Stephen B. Minor ack. before James Archer, J. Q,, Mch. 29, 1812. Recorded Apr 1, 1812.

p. 125. June 13, 1804. William Smith, of Claiborne Co., and Ann, his wife, to Philip
Garagthy and Richard O'Reilly, of Natchez, for $4000, tract on Bayou de la Cypriera
which empties itself into the Mississippi a short distance above Petty Gulf and
within Claiborne Co., 800 acres, adj. Peter B. Bruin, and granted to William Smith
by the Sp. Govt. in 1795. Signed: William Smith, Ann (x) Smith. Wit: Thos. Jordan,
David Smith. Ack. by Wm. Smith before Daniel Vertner, 4 Mch. 1813, and Ann Smith
21 Apr. 1813. The original deed and probate thereof in this office, 24 Apr. 1813.
(Signature of the Justice illegible.)

p. 132. Feb 7, 1813. Joseph McRaven and Peggy, his wife, and John Norton, all of
Claiborne Co., Miss. Ter., to John W. Hamilton and James Hart, both of Tennessee,
for $3000, 500 acres adj. Indian boundary line, known as Smith's Old Stand, or
Red Bluffs, certificate issued to William Smith as preemption claim. Wit: John B.
Willis, Noble Osborn, L. D. Carson.

p. 358. 11 July 1814. Stephen B. Minor and Nancy, his wife, of Claiborne Co., Miss.
Ter., and William B. Minor, of same. Whereas: William Brocus, Senr., deceased, late
of sd Co. and Ter., by last will, devised to Stephen B. Minor and William B. Minor,
after the death of his daughter, Ann, the plantation and tract of land whereon the
said William Brocus resided before and at the time of his death, containing 1000
acres, etc., and whereas the said testator devised one other tract of land unto the
sd Stephen B. Minor and William B. Minor, of 1000 acres, which sd Minor wishes to
sell to Samuel Richardson, of Adams Co., and it being necessary in order to make
a good and valid deed to said Richardson , of the said William B. Minor becoming
a party to the deed to sd Richardson, and for one dollar, the sd Stephen B. Minor
acquits the said tract of 1000 acres whereon sd Brocus, Senr., lived and the same
in which he devised a life estate to his daughter Ann. Signed Stephen B. Minor,
Ann Minor. Wit: S. D. Carson, Sam'l. Richardson, Robt. Steel, H. Harman. Nancy,
wife of Stephen B. Minor, ack. before H. Harman, J. Q. 11 July 1814.

p. 404. 5 June 1814. Levi Thompson and Mary, his wife, to Richmond Sheffield,
all of Claiborne Co., Miss. Ter., for $200, 640 acres on Bayou Pierre in Claiborne
Co., confirmed to the heirs of William Thompson, dec'd., by Commrs. West of the
Pearl River, the said Levi being one of the heirs of William Thompson, dec.'d.
Levi and Mary Thompson before H. Harman, J. Q., 25 June 1814.

p. 417. 12 Dec. 1814. Hezekiah Harman, tax collector, to Jeremiah and David Hunt,
surviving exrs. of Abijah Hunt, for $7.80, a tract on South Fork of Bayou Pierre,
chargeable as the property of Jesse Griffin or the heirs of John Smith, dec'd., as
adv. in Natchez newspaper, Sept. 1, 1814, being the land whereon the late Jesse
Griffin lived and died.

Book D

p. 406. By virtue of an order of execution by the Superior Court of Claiborne
County, in favor of Waterman Crane against John Peck for $500.96, July 15, 1814.
Joseph Briggs, Sheriff, sold two lots of 500 acres each on the north side of Bayou
Pierre, on the west side of 500 acres claimed by Silas Crane, and north of Thomas
Barnes and Geo. W. Humphreys, beginning at line of the heirs of John Hartley, dec'd.,
within the survey called Lyman mandamus, as property of John Peck; due notices
having been given by law, by public sale, Aug. 24, 1814, to the highest bidder,
James Crane, for $92.

p. 430. 30 April 1815. John Peck, of Boston, Mass., by Rob't. Williams, atty.-in-fact,
to Israel Loring, of Claiborne., for $925, 185 acres on north fork of Bayou Pierre,
being a tract where Andrew Mundell used to live and a part of 9000 acres conveyed
by Thaddeus Lyman to Oliver Lyman, Thompson Lyman, Eleanor Lyman and Experience
Lyman, by deeds, said 9000 acres being part of the Lyman Mandamus and conveyed
by Oliver Lyman to sd John Peck. Wit: Chas. Defrance, J. G. Clarke.

p. 432. May 2, 1815. Wm. Scott, of Claiborne Co., Miss. Ter., to Samuel Dorsey, of
Concordia Parish, La., for $1563, 556 acres in Claiborne Co., adj. John Hartley's
on the south side of the North Fork of Bayou Pierre, conveyed by John Milliken and
Mary, his wife, to Samuel Fry, May 14, 1810, and from Fry to Robert Scott, 4 July,
1812 and by deed from Robert Scott to Wm. Scott. Signed. Wit: J. G. Clarke, John
Scott, Jr.

p. 434. 6 March 1812. Chattle Mortgage. Stephen B. Minor to John Gibson, for $200,
4 cherry tables, one cupboard and 3 beds with their furniture. (signed) Stephen B.
Minor. Wit: J. H. Moore. Ack. by Minor before J. Wood, J. Q. 10 Aug. 1815.

p. 434-5. 26 March, 1814. Bill of sale. Stephen B. Minor to John Gibson, both of
Claiborne Co., Miss. Ter., for $125, one negro man, Alpha, abt. 50 years old. (signed)
Stephen B. Minor. Wit: Seth Robinson. Ack. by Stephen B. Minor before J. Wood, J. Q.
10 Aug. 1815. Recorded same day.

Book E.

p. 1. May 2, 1815. Joseph Briggs, of Claiborne Co., Miss. Ter., to Samuel Dorsey, of
Louisiana, 199 acres which sd Briggs held by deed from John Peck, of Boston, Mass.,
by his agent and atty. in fact, Robert Williams, in Claiborne Co., on the north side
of Bayou Pierre, described in Bk D, pp. 26 and 329. Ann Briggs relinquished her dower.
Signed Wit: D. T. January, Thos. Barnes.

p. 36. Dec. 16, 1815. William B. Minor, Ann Brashears and Elizabeth C., wife of William
B. Minor, of Claiborne Co., to William Willis, of Concordia Parish, Louisiana, at present
of the City of Natchez, for $3000, 1000 acres on the South Fork of Bayou Pierre,
bounded on one side by lands granted to Gibson Clark and now occupied by the heirs
of Elias Barnes and by lands granted to William Brocus, also by Bayou Pierre,
being the same tract on which William Brocus resided at the time of his death and
gave to Ann Brashears in her lifetime and after her death to her children, Stephen
B. and William B. Minor, being a Spanish grant and recorded in Written Evidences,
page 135 by John Girault, translator, and dated 18 June, 1792. (signed) William B.
Minor, Ann (x) Brashears, Elizabeth C. Minor. Wit: Wit: Gabriel H. Kehan, Abram Barnes.
Ack. by Elizabeth C. Minor, wife of William B. Minor, before Thomas Barnes, J. Q.
6 March, 1816. Rec. Mch. 6, 1816. D. T. January, Clerk.

p. 40. 16 Dec. 1815. William B. Minor and Elizabeth, his wife, of Claiborne Co., for
$800, 400 acres on South Fork of Bayou Pierre, b. by lands of William Brocus and
those of Thomas Creighton, granted to Wm. Brocus, 28 Feb. 1795 by Spanish Govt.
Signed: William B. Minor, Elizabeth C. Minor. Wit: Abram Barnes, James Beecham.
Thomas Barnes, J. Q.

Book E.

p. 68. 11 July 1814. William B. Minor, of Claiborne Co., to Stephen B. Minor, of same, quit claim deed to 1000 arpens, on North Fork of Bayou Pierre, gr. by Sp. Govt. to Wm. Brocus, 20 Jany., 1795, also my right to following negro slaves, (two, named). Signed Wm. B. Minor. Wit: Jos. H. Moore, Samuel Richardson. Prov. by Joseph Moore, 11 April, 1816, bef. H. Harman, J. Q. and filed.

p. 176. 24 Oct. 1816. John Smith and Dorothy, his wife, of Parish of Concordia, Louisiana, to Thomas Freeland, of Claiborne Co., Miss., for $3000, 232 acres, tract bounded on north by land claimed by James Corbet, on south by David Smith, on east and west by Evans and Overaker. Signed. John Smith, Doretha(x) Smith. Wit: John Hopper, H. Harman. Ack. 24 Oct. 1816.

p. 182. 16 Dec. 1816. Robt. Scott and Mary, his wife, of Jessamine Co., Ky. to Samuel Dorsey, of Claiborne Co., for $1563, 576 acres on North Fork of Bayou Pierre, being the same tract conveyed by John Millikin and Mary, his wife to Samuel Fry, 14 May 1810, and by admrs of Samuel Frye, to Robert Scott, 4 July, 1812.

p. 186. 13 Feb. 1817. James Corbet and Pharaba, his wife, of Claiborne Co., Miss. Ter., to Thos and Augusta Freeland, of same, for $285, 57 acres, conveyed to sd James Corbet by Wm. Smith by deed of gift. Signed by both. Wit: H. Harman, John Hoppe. Ack. by both, wife examined separately. Filed Feb. 15, 1817.

p. 217. 11 Sept. 1817. Elijah Smith, of Adams Co., and Mary, his wife, to David Hunt, of Jefferson Co., for $10,000, a tract on the North Fork of Bayou Pierre. (see p. 296 below). Wit: L. Harding, Israel Loring.

p. 223. 14 Feb. 1817. David Smith and Mary, his wife, of Claiborne Co., to Robert Cochran, for $428, 300 acres, bounded on south by David McFarland, west Bruin-Burgh plantation, north by Augustus Freeland and east Mount plantation. David Smith, Mary(x)Smith. Wit: P. A. Candova, John Lombard. Ack. Feb. 17, 1817.

p. 296. 11 Sept 1817. Elijah Smith and Mary, his wife, and David Hunt and Ann, his wife, all of Miss. Ter., to Daniel Burnet of Claiborne Co., for $5000, paid by Burnet, an undivided one-half of 1000 French acres on North Fork of Bayou Pierre, in Claiborne Co., at a place called Grindstone Ford, being the tract of 1000 acres gr. to said Daniel Burnet by the Spanish Govt., 31 Aug. 1791 and the sd moiety or one-half of which was conveyed to George Humphreys by sd Daniel Burnet, 27 June 1796, which sd moiety was conveyed to Abijah Hunt by sd Geo. W. Humphreys and wife, Sarah, 9 Nov. 1805, and afterwards conveyed by Jeremiah and David Hunt, surviving exrs of Abijah Hunt, dec'd., to Elijah Smith by deed, May 1, 1816, and by Elijah and Mary, his wife to David Hunt, 2 July 1816. Signed by all. Wit: Josiah Simpson, Ann Simpson. Ack. by wife separately. Rec. 20 Feb. 1819.

p. 338. 21 Jany. 1818. James Crane to Mary Mundell, for $1000, 500 acres on North Fork of Bayou Pierre, adj. heirs of John Hartley. Signed. Wit: G. W. Humphreys, D. G. Humphreys and James Boyer.

p. 395. 1 Sept. 1818. Samuel Dorsey to John Thompson, both of Claiborne Co., 300 acres in Cape Girardeau, Ter. of Missouri, known as the Harris Austin tract. Signed Samuel Dorsey. Wit: Amos Whiting, P. A. Hughes. Filed, 25 Sept. 1818. P. A. Van Dorn, Clerk.

Book F.

p. 315. 16 Dec. 1820. Isaac Powers and Sarah, his wife, of Claiborne Co., Miss.
to Henry G. Johnson, of same, for $64.50, 26 acres in sd county, part of 124 acres
purchased by Isaac Powers, Dec. 18, 1815. Signed by both and ack. before Walter
Leake, Judge of Supreme and Superior Court for the Second District, 16 Dec. 1820.

p. 386. Patent from the United States to Darius and Charles Hamilton, of Claiborne
Co., Miss., of 160 acres, Oct. 10, 1820

Book G.

p. 68. Nov. 3, 1822. John W. Hamilton and James Hart, of Sumner Co., Tenn., made
bond, 30 June 1817, for $2000, secured by Davenport Wiseman, then of Claiborne Co.,
now deceased. Col. Ralph Regan, executor of D. Wiseman, paid two obligations and
Davenport Wiseman disposed of tract in will, and John W. Hamilton confirms title
to Regan, executor of said Wiseman, to tract of 280 acres on the waters of the Big
Black. Signed J. W. Hamilton. Wit: Stephen Tyler, L. C. Higgins. Ack. by Higgins
before W. Carson, J. Q. C. C. June 28, 1822. Jas Cornell, Clk.

p. 122. Nov. 3, 1822. John W. Thompson and Thompson White, agreement,
Claiborne Co., John W. Thompson purchased of Wm. White, Nelson White, Joseph
White and Patrick Brown, all heirs of Thomas White, three-fourths of whole estate,
and Thompson White has purchased of Ralph Regan his interest and one-half of
Davenport' Wiseman's interest. They divide land. Signed by John W. Thompson
and Thompson White. Wit: James M. Bradford, James Cornell. Ack. by both,
17 Feb. 1823, before James Cornell, J. P. Filed same day, Jas. Cornell, Clk.

p. 171. 22 April 1820, John W. Thompson and wife, Mary, to Benj. Smith, for $5600,
400 acres on South Fork of Bayou Pierre, bounded north and west by lands of Nelson
White and south and east by lands of John Thompson and Thompson White. Signed
John Thomson, Mary Thomson. Ack. 22 April, 1823 by both before James Cornell, J. P.
Filed same day by Jas. Cornell, Clerk.

p. 208. 7 June 1823. Reuben Marshall and Rachel, his wife, to Benj. Beard, both of
Claiborne Co., for $300, 93 acres, bounded by lands of heirs of Abel Eastman, dec'd.,
set aside to Rachel Marshall, wife of Reuben Marshall, heir-at-law of Abel Eastman.
Reuben(x)Marshall. Rachel Marshall. Wit: James Siddon, Amos Rundell. Ack. by
both before James Crane, J. P.

p. 362. March 26, 1824. Samuel Dorsey, for love and affection to son, John Thompson
Dorsey, all interest in firm of Dorsey and Applegate. Ack. by Sam'l. Dorsey and Geo.
P. Applegate.

p. 360. Mch. 26, 1824. Agreement. Partnership to be formed for mercantile druggist
house, in Port Gibson, to be continued three years by Samuel Dorsey and Geo. P. Applegate. Samuel Dorsey to furnish stock of medecines, etc., valued at $1775: George
Applegate to attend and manage business without charge and Samuel Dorsey obligates
himself that his son, Thompson Dorsey, shall attend said business without charge.
Both signed. Wit: B. W. Johnstan, John H. Esty.

Book H.

p. 114. 19 Mch. 1825. Benjamin Beard and Salome, his wife, of Claiborne Co., Miss.
to Wm. Kinnason, of same, for $500, 86 acres in sd county, land of which the late
Abel Eastman died possessed, which land was set off as a dower to his widow, the
party of the first part, by an order of the Orphans Court. Signed Benj. Beard,
Salome Beard. Wit: Wm. Kinnason, James Crane. Ack. by both, separately, 17 Mch. 1825.

Book H.

p. 116. March 19, 1825. David Eastman and Charlotte, his wife, to Wm. Kinnason, all of Claiborne Co., for $50, land set off to widow of Abel Eastman. Wit:James Crane, Benj. Beard. Ack. by David H. Eastman and Charlotte Eastman before James Crane, same date.

p. 222. (Fees paid $2. 27). Aug. 23, 1825. Cyrus Hamilton and Margaret, his wife, to Darius Hamilton and Nancy, his wife, Deborah Hartley, Hugh Mathews and Annie, his wife, to Charles Hamilton, for $600, each of the parties being entitled to one share, or $100, and Hercules Hamilton to two shares or $200, confirm and set over to Charles Hamilton 300 arpens of land in Claiborne Co., the same on which Chas. Hamilton now resides, formerly the property of Jesse Hamilton, late of Jefferson County, Miss., bounded on the north by vacant lands, on west by Bayou Pierre, on south by heirs of Francis Nailer, dec'd., and by lands of James Davenport, junr., dec'd. Signed Cyrus Hamilton, Margaret(x)Hamilton, Hercules Hamilton, Hetty(x) Hamilton, Hugh Mathews, Anna Mathews, Deborah(x)Hartley, Darius Hamilton, Ann Hamilton. Cyrus and Margaret examined apart, and Deborah Hartley ack. Aug. 23, 1825:Hercules and Hetty Hamilton, Hugh and Anna Mathews ack. Sept. 25, 1825. Darius and Ann Hamilton ack .... 1826. Recorded Jany. 21, 1826.

p. 228. Jany. 1826. John T. Dorsey and Ann C., his wife, to Abram K. Shaifer, all of Claiborne Co., for $2500, Lot 3. Both signed. Wit: Samuel Hoite. Wit:Geo. P. Applegate. (John Thomson Dorsey and Ann C. Hoits were married May 26, 1825.)

p. 357. June 26, 1822. Mordecai Baldwin and Sarah, his wife, for $25, to John W. Hamilton, of Sumner County, Tenn., all claim in 499 acres. Wit: Raymond Robinson, William M. Leake. Ack. by Raymond Robinson, 4th July 1826 beforeS. P. mcGee. Recorded 4th September, 1826. Wm. David, Clerk.

Book I

p. 1. April 27, 1826. A. K. Shaiffer, Sheriff, to Thomas Freeland, by virtue of judgment issued from the Clerk's Office of Circuit Court, of Claiborne Co., 8 Nov. 1825, in favor of C. Haring for L. Lassassier, for $120. 66 with 8% interest, until paid, against the goods and chattels of Nicholas H. Christian, execution on all right, title and interest, until paid, against the goods and chattels of his deceased father's estate, the property of sd Nicholas H. Christian, in Claiborne Co. on James Creek, adj. lands of Waterman Crane and Thomas Freeland. After due notice, the Sheriff did on 17 Apr. 1820 expose to sale all the interest in said land to the highest bidder, same being Thomas Freeland, for $60. The deed to all interest of Nicholas H. Christian to afsd lands. Signed by A. K. Shaiffer, Sheriff.

p. 60. Jany. 17, 1822. It is hereby certified that Benj. Beard, of Warren County, 11 Jany. 1819 purchased 560 acres offered for sale at Washington for $2. 00 per acre. The sd Benj. Beard, availing himself of the act of Congress, of Mch. 2, 1821, for purchase of land before July 1st, 1821, has surrendered the original certificate, dated June 27, 1821, in which he has relinquished part of sd section and requested a further credit on the northwest part, 202 acres, at the rate amounting to $404, of which $280 being more than one-half and less than three fourths, the remainder to be paid in sex equal instalments. Signed. B. R. Grayson, Register. //p. 61. Benj. Beard and wife relinquish the above to Reuben Marshall for $600. Signed Benja. Beard, Salome Beard. Ack. March 5, 1822 in Warren Co., before Jacob Hyland, by Benj. Beard. // p. 62. Reuben Marshall and Rachel, his wife, to A. D. S. Dillingham, all of Claiborne Co., 3 Dec. 1824, for $1800. Ack. separately before Daniel Burnet, J. P. // pp. 63-4. A. D. S. Dillingham and Nancy, his wife, to William Watkins, for $4000, all claim to above certificate, 4 Nov. 1826. Both signed. Ack. separately before Daniel Burnet, J. P. 20 Dec. 1826. Rec. Dec. 25, 1826.

Book I

p. 301. 12 June 1827. John Hendrick, of Claiborne Co., Miss., guardian of my children, Rachel Hedrick, Gibson C.(lark) Hedrick, John H. Hedrick, Laura Jane Hedrick, Martha Ann Hedrick and William C(lark) Hedrick. A chattel mortgage on cotton and corn crop to William Clark, of Jefferson Co., Miss., for $600, at 8% interest. Signed John Hedrick. Wit: Lionel Fletcher, Samuel Hoit. Ack. before Samuel Hoit, J. P., 12 June 1827. Rec. same day. Wm. Davis, Clk. (John Hedrick was the son of Peter Hedrick and his daughter, Laura Jane Hedrick was the first wife of Henry Goodloe Johnson Powers.)

p. 423. 2nd Jany. 1822. Nancy Corbett to John Jones, bond for $500. The condition that Nancy Corbett does transfer and relinquish all her right and title in an entry made in the town of Washington, in the name of William Truitt and Nancy Corbet, to her infant daughter, Susan Corbett, as the law would direct. Nancy(x) Corbett, Wit: Thos. W. Cogan, Edward R. J. Almitt. Proved by Cogan, 17 Oct. 1827.

p. 424. 22 Jany. 1827. John Gurley and Elizabeth, his wife, to Joseph Beard, for $25, 37 acres. Both signed with a mark. Wit: John A. Barnes, John Johnson. Ack. 26 Feb. 1827.

Book K.

p. 14. 26 April 1827. John W. Hamilton and Rocha, his wife, of Claiborne Co., to William H. Chambers, of Adams Co., Miss., for $10,000, 1000 acres in Claiborne County, described by Section and Range, etc. Signed J. W. Hamilton, Rocha Hamilton. Wit: John A. Quitman, Wm. B. Griffith. Ack. by John W. Hamilton, 30 April, 1827, before H. Tooley, J. P., Adams Co., Miss. Ack. by Rocha Hamilton before Nath. W. Williams, J. C. C. Law and Equity for Smith Co., Tennessee, 27 Nov. 1827. Rec. 3rd January, 1828, Wm. David, Clk.

p. 62. 15 May, 1827. Thos. W. Cogan and wife, Rebecka, to Joseph Elmore, all of Claiborne Co., for $600, 80 acres, west of Pearl River, gr. Cogan in 1823. Wit: D. McCall, Aaron Ash. Ack. 15 May, 1827, before Dugald McCall, J. P. Ack. by signers 20 Feb. 1828 before Sam'l. Hoit, J. P. Rec. 15 March, 1828. Jno. Jennings, Clk.

p. 77. 16 Jany. 1828. Joseph Beard and Sarah, his wife, to John Siddon and William Beale, all of Claiborne Co., for $50, 25 acres. Joseph Beard signed, Sary Beard used mark. Wit: Benj Beard, Thos. Stanfield.

p. 95. Feb. 20, 1828. Horace Carpenter and Martha, his wife, to Robt. S. Hamilton, all of Port Gibson, Miss., sell Town lot opposite Fair Street, being the same lot formerly owned by Mathew T. Hines. Signed Horace Carpenter, Martha W. Carpenter. Ack. 20, Feb. 1828 before Samuel Hoit, J. P. Recorded 15 Mch. 1828, John Jennings, D. C.

p. 219. 29 April, 1823. Levin Disharon to Ann Hamilton, widow of the late Darias Hamilton, dec., all of Claiborne Co., Miss., for $4,000, 500 acres in the northwest corner of a tract known as the "Lyman Mandamus". Signed. Ack. 29th April, 1828 before B. W. Johnston, J. P. Rec. Oct. 8, 1828. Wm. Davis, Clk.

p. 298. 16 April, 1820. Claiborne Co., Miss., for $1000, 500 acres on the North Fork of Bayou Pierre, adj. land of John Hartley's heirs, and James Crane's land, to A. D. S. Dillingham and Abijah H. Mundell, to be held by them as tenants in common. Signed Polly Mundell. Wit: S. D. Carson, Margaret Dillingham, Joseph M. Mundell. Ack. by Stephen D. Carson 23 Jany. 1829, before Samuel Hoit, J. P. Rec. Jany. 23, 1829. Wm. David, Clerk.

p. 402. 13 Apr. 1828. Campbell McCay and Catherine, his wife, to Robert McKay and Francis Murdock, $300 for hire of two women for 18 months, beginning Feb. 1829 and ending 4 Aug. 1830. Wit: S. Hoit.

p. 435. 16 May, 1829. Tom Simmons and Martha, his wife, to Jeremiah Thomson, for $400 paid by sd Thomson, hath sold to him 80 acres in North East corner of Section No. 21. Signed by both. Wit: S. Hoit. Ack. by both before S. Hoit, Martha separately, same date. Rec. June 6, 1829. Wm. David, Clerk.

Book K

p, 420. March 28, 1829. Harrison E. Watson and wife, Mary Watson, of Claiborne Co.,
for $1.00 and twenty bales of good merchantable cotton to average 400 pounds, each,
to be delivered to us on a suitable landing on Bayou Pierre, Nov. 1, 1829, convey to
Milford Hunter, of same county, all right, title, etc. that Harrison E. Watson and Mary,
his wife, (late Mary Hamilton) as her dower in and to the real estate of the late
Charles Hamilton, dec'd., so long as we are capable in law of selling the same.
Signed H. E. Watson, Mary Watson. Wit: Nicholas McDougall. Ack. by the above,
Mary being examined separately, 28 Mch. 1829. Rec. Apr. 30, 1829.

p. 475. 27 Dec. 1828. Indenture between Eleazar Tharp and Phebe, his wife, of
Claiborne Co., Miss., and Ann Hamilton of Hinds Co., Miss. For $1000, all those
certain tracts and parcels of land lying in Hinds County in the East half of SE
Quarter of Sec. 11, T14 North, Range 5, 79.47 acres and 67.44 and 134.87 acres,
etc. Signed Eleazar Tharp, Phebe (x) Tharp. Ack. 7 Dec. 1828, before Nichs. Mc
Dougald, J. P. Rec. Aug. 15, 1829. Wm. David, Clk.

p. 526. Nov. 4, 1829. Jeremiah Thompson and Emily, his wife, to David Humphreys,
for $450, 80 acres in Claiborne Co.. Signed Jeremiah Thomson, Emily Thomson.
Ack. in Court. (Jeremiah was a grandson of Jeremiah Thomson of Warren Co., Miss.
Emily was a Bullock.)

Book L.
p. 26. 10 Oct. 1829. Levi Eastman, of Warren Co., to Benj. Beard, of Claiborne Co.,
for $100, 93 acres in Claiborne Co. bounded by Lot No. 3 and on the south by
vacant lands, as divided by Daniel Burnet and other commissioners appointed by
the Orphans Court of Claiborne Co. to divide the lands of Abel Eastman. Signed
Levi Eastman. Wit: Joshua Rundell, William Beale. Ack. 10 Oct. 1829.

Book M.
p. 40. 23 Aug. 1830. Abijah H. Mundell, of Claiborne Co., to Dennis Burns, for
$3500, 250 acres in upper division of Lyman Mandamus, bound on south by George
Wilson Humphreys, east John A. Barnes, north Isaac Ross, Jr., west lands late the
property of Thos. Marble, it being one-half of the tract sold to James Crane,
Aug. 24, 1814, also negro Nelson, about 17, Lucy about 17, with stock of hogs, etc.
(Abijah Hunt Mundell was the son of Andrew Mundell and his second wife, Mary(Polly)
Smith, widow of Vachel Dillingham, Jr., of Kentucky, and daughter of Maj. David
Smith, formerly of the Hermitage plantation on Bayou Pierre.)

Book N.
p. 12. Ezra Marble, 7 Feb. 1833, for love and affection and $5.00, to Philema White,
Lot No. 1, Square No. 7 in Grand Gulf.

p. 14. Feb. 7, 1833. Deed. Ezra Marble, of Claiborne Co., to Amanda M. Marble,
Frances H. Marble, Ezra E. Marble, and Amelia V. Marble, children of said Ezra
Marble, and Edwin M. Strother and Covington B. Strother, his grandchildren, lots
in Grand Gulf. Amanda M. Marble, Lot No. 2, Sq. 15; Frances H., Lot No. 3; Ezra E.
Lot No. 6; Amelia Lot No. 7; Edwin M. Strother and Covington Strother, Lot. No. 10.

Book O.
p. 120. Milford Hunter and Susan, his wife, of Claiborne Co., for $700, to C. W.
Muncastle and Co., of same, land bounded on north vacant lands in Mississippi
swamp; on east lands belonging to James Davenport; south, land of Drewry W.
Tucker; on west by Bayou Pierre, being the dower of Polly Hamilton alias Polly
Watson, which dower is supposed to include dwelling house, the mill and gin and
all appurtenances, Feb. 1, 1833. Signed Milford Hunter, Susan Hunter.

Book O

p.194. Jany.3,1831. John Rail, of Warren Co., to Abijah Mundell, of Claiborne Co., for $500, 80 acres in Claiborne, Lot No.7, Sec.28, T13, R2E. (Same township with lands of John Tomson, adj. Range.)

p.219. 23 Feb.1835. Robt. McCay and Eliza McCay, his wife, of Claiborne Co., to Richard White, $200, land in Claiborne, metes and bounds given. Both sign. Ack. in Court by McKay.

p.241. March 2.1835. Robt. McCay and Eliza, his wife, to Richard Ingram and. wife, Susanna, for $6,000, lots in Port Gibson bought of Passmore Harpes. No witnesses. Ack.in Court.

p.521. 29 Aug.1835. Deed from Hugh M.Dees, Trustee for J.B.Fairchild & Co., in absence of Elias Bridges, Co-Trustee, to Robert Jones, all of town of Grand Gulf, Claiborne Co., State of Miss., for $5180, for upper half of Lot 3, Square One of Town of Grand Gulf. Signed. Hugh M.Dees. Ack. by signer 29 Aug.1835 before C.J.Jeffries, J.P. Recorded Sept.2, 1835. S.O.Bridewell, Clk.

Book P

p.182. 23 March, 1836. Deed from Robert Jones and wife, Mary B.Jones, of Town of Grand Gulf, in County of Claiborne, Miss., to Joseph Chapman, of Copiah Co., Miss., for $7200, the upper half of Lot 3, Square One, in Town of Grand Gulf and extending back to the Mississippi River, having erected thereon a two story brick house, frame warehouse, etc. Signed Robert Jones, Mary B.Jones. Ack. by signers 23 Mch.1836 before Lewis Crowley, J.P. Rec.24 Mch.1836. J.W.Wetherall, Clk.

p.301. May 12,1836. Llewellyn Price, Sr., and Margaret, his wife, to Mathew Boils, tract originally gr by Sp. Govt. to Martin and Ralph Price and by them conveyed to Llewellyn Price. Signed Llewellyn Price. Margaret Price.

p.485. 21st June 1836. Deed from Robert Jones and wife, Mary B.Jones, of Claiborne Co., Miss. to I.C.Curtis, of same, for $3,300, part of Lots 10, 9, and 2, Square 4, Grand Gulf, Claiborne Co., Miss., adj. ground deeded to George Lake and P.H.Petty by William M.Fairchild and wife, Mahala. Signed Robert Jones, Mary B.Jones. Ack. by signer, 20 June 1836 before Gilbert D.Gere, Clk. of Circuit Court of Covington County, Miss. Rec.20 July 1836. M.O.Hopkins, D.C.

p.505. Robt.McCay of Town of Port Gibson, for $18.00, to Israel Loring, of same, one half-acre adj. town, forming a triangle, Sept.1,1830. No wit. Ack. in Court.

Book Q.

p.334-5. Samuel Rusk and wife, Myra Rusk, to F.W. and D.H.Turpin, 31 July, 1837. Samuel Rusk, heir and distributee in right of his wife, Myra Rusk, of the estate of John Thompson, dec'd, and Myra Rusk, late Myra Thompson, heir of John Thompson, dec'd., of the State of Louisiana, to Frances W.Turpin and David H.Turpin, of Claiborne, for $3500, quit claim to his estate right in plantation of John Thompson, six miles above the Grand Gulf, lying immediately on the Mississippi, bounded on NE by lands on which Henry Shaifer formerly lived, on east by John B.Thacher, etc., 700 acres. (The name should have been spelled Thomson as the family was a branch of the large Thomson Family of Louisa Co., Va.)

Book R.

p.69. Walter Strother and Prudence G., his wife, to Jeremiah Thompson, of Claiborne Co., 80 acres, for $100. Signed by both. Wit: N.McDougall. Aug.16, 1836.

Book R

p. 193. Whereas the late Charles Hamilton, dec'd., possessed certain lands in Claiborne Co., 1/4 of Sec. 15, T. 12, R1E and part of Sec. 10, of same township, Amos Riley, by intermarriage with the late Lucy Ann Hamilton, now Lucy Ann Riley, of Jefferson Co., Kentucky, is justly entitled to a share of the above described lands as heirs and distributees of said Chas. Hamilton, dec'd., in consideration of $420 convey to Maria L. Whiting, administratrix, and George Lake, administrator, of Amos Whiting, dec'd., the whole of their individual interest in the above described land. Jan. 6, 1838. No. wit. Signed Amos Riley, Lucy Ann Riley. Ack. by Amos and Lucy Ann Riley at Grand Gulf, Jan. 9, 1838.

p. 330. March 30, 1838. Lemuel Gustine and Sophia, his wife, late Sophia Thompson, devisee of John Thompson, dec'd., of Claiborne Co., to John Byrd Thrasher. of Port Gibson, for $4320, all right, title, etc., as devisees of John Thomson, deceased, late of this county, being one-fifth interest in the following tracts, (two, totalling 364 acres) granted to John Thomson, 24 May 1831, all in Claiborne Co., above mouth of Big Black, which undivided one-fifth is 72.88 acres. Signed: Lemuel Gustine, Sophia Gustine. Wit: E. A. McLean, J. W. Fisher.

Book S.

p. 199. Sept. 1838. Amos Riley and Lucy Ann, his wife, of Jefferson Co., Ky., to Thos. Berry, of Claiborne Co., for $400, land in Claiborne Co., formerly owned by Chas. Hamilton, dec'd., bounded on n. vacant lands, w. Bayou Pierre; s. Francis Nailor; e. lands of heirs of James Davenport, Jr., dec'd., 300 arpens, one-half of above mentioned tract being hereby intended to be conveyed, it being the part which descended to said Lucy Ann Riley, formerly Lucy Ann Hamilton, as one of the heirs of Chas. Hamilton, dec'd. Signed Amos Riley, Lucy Ann Riley. No wit. State of Ky., City of Louisville, Frederick A. Keys, Mayor of City of Louisville, certifies that Amos and Lucy Riley acknowledge the foregoing. Oct. 15, 1838. Rec. Jany. 5, 1839.

p. 275. John H. Thomson, quit claim deed to Sophia Thomson, both of Claiborne Co., for $6,000, in hand paid. All my right, title, interest, claim, etc., to all the undivided estate of my father, John Thomson, dec'd., to wit: land in Claiborne Co., T13, Sec. 22, R1E, bounded on east by Henry Shaifer; south J. B. Thrasher, west Permelius Briscoe, north Mississippi River; also slaves, Jack, Dave and Flora, and all property whatsoever from estate. Signed John H. Thomson. Nov. 13, 1835. Recorded Feb. 27, 1839

Book W

p. 31. May, 1844. Cynthia Thomson, devisee and heir-at-law of John Thomson, dec'd, of Claiborne Co., Miss., to John B. Thrasher, of Port Gibson, for $2200, all her right, title, claim and interest, as heir of John Thomson, dec'd., being one-fifth part of the following tracts of land: Fractional Sec. 23, T13, R1E, original survey (Lots 1 and 2 in Sec. 23, T13 according to resurvey, 4 Jany. 1828) 252 acres, also Lot 1 Sec 22, T13, R1E, 111.68 acres, etc. Sihned Cynthia Thomson. Ack. in Court same date.

p. 433. Robt. McCay, of Pike Co., title bond to Wm. O. Kelly and Henry O. Kelly, of Claiborne Co., $7000 bond, 10 Mch. 1845, to sell Wm. and Henry property in Port Gibson on Suburd St. Mary, adjoining a lot belonging to the Planters Bank, Walnut Street. Signed Robert McCay. No. wit. Ack. in Claiborne Co., March 11, 1843 by Robert McCay.

Book Y

p. 405. 6 Apr. 1848. Wm. M. Quin and Bythel Haynes, in right of his wife, Delia
Haynes, exrs. of last will and testament of Robert McCay, late of Pike Co., Miss.,
dec'd., to Henry T. Ellet, for $400, lot adjoining Port Gibson, 15 acres, excepting
one-half acre conveyed to Israel Loring. Signed by both. Ack. in Pike County by
Wm. W. Quin. Ack. in Amite Co., by Bythell Haynes, one of the exrs. of last will
and test. of Robt. McCay, dec'd. late of Pike Co.

Book Y

p. 485. Trussy Bethea and Malinda, Nov. 11, 1848, for $2500, to R. C. Hutchinson,
an undivided one-half of following lots of land in Port Gibson, (description),
deeded June 15, 1846 to Richard Harding and wife to Philip and Trussy Bethea,
to have and to hold. Signed Trussy Bethea, Malinda Bethea.

p. 488. Philip Bethea and wife, Missouri, repeat the sale of their half of the
above property.

Book CC

p. 167. 29th Sept. 1855. Gift deed from Isaac Powers and Sarah, his wife, of
Claiborne Co., to Thomas Owen, W. J. Lum, Henry G. J. Powers, Isaac Powers, Richard
Harding, Orville R. Early and Samuel McClellan, Trustees, in trust that they and
their successors shall build thereon and continue thereon a house or place of
worship for the use of the Methodist Episcopal Church South. Signed: Isaac
Powers, Sarah Powers. Ack. by both before Samuel McClellan, member of Board
of Police of Claiborne County, Miss., 24 Oct. 1855. Recorded Dec. 3rd, 1855.
James A. Gage, Clk. (This acreage was the building site of the "Red Brick"
Methodist Church in Rocky Springs, Claiborne County, Miss. The church is still
standing and in use.)

Book KK

p. 368. 1st Feb. 1873. Matilda J. Lake, Geo. A. Lake, Alice Smith and Stephen Smith
of Claiborne Co., Miss., deed to John A. Jones and Milton R. Jones, of Hinds Co.,
for $13,500, 1075 acres in Claiborne Co., b. north by lands of William Ewell and
Wm. Ross; on south by north bank of the North Fork of Bayou Pierre and lands of
Charles B. Clark, Dr. W. P. Hughes and Jonathan McCaleb, deceased; on east by
Hermitage plantation; on west by lands conveyed by parties of first to L. N. Baldwin
and L. Y. Berry by deed dated June 17, 1872, etc., all in T12, R4E. Signed: Matilda
J. Lake, George A. Lake, Alica Smith, Stephen F. Smith. Ack. by signers 1st Feb, 1873
before G. W. Harvey, J. P. Recorded 15 March, 1873, Solomon Unger, Clk.

p. 608. 19 September, 1873. Susannah Powell, of Claiborne Co., Miss., deeds to
Olive B. Harper, wife of John J. Harper, of same, for $2,000, 321.71 acres (by Sec.,
Township and Range) in Claiborne Co. Signed Susannah P. Powell. Ack. by signer,
23 Sept. 1873, before A. J. Brown, J. P. Rec. Sept. 24, 1873, by T. C. Borum, D. C.
Solomon Unger, Clk.

Book VV

p. 337. 1st Dec. 1879. Jno. A. Jones, and A. M. Jones, his wife, M. R. Jones and wife, E. B. Jones,
of Hinds and Claiborne Cos., Miss., deed to M. R. Jones, of Claiborne Co., Miss.,
for $13,000, 1075 acres in T12, R4E, (See Bk. KK, p. 368). Signed: Jno. A. Jones,
A. M. Jones, M. R. Jones. Ack. by Jno. A. Jones and A. M. Jones, 25 Feb. 1881 before
Geo. Robertson, Mayor of Utica, Miss., and Ex Officio J. P. Ack. by M. R. Jones,
3rd March 1881 before A. K. Jones, Clerk of Claiborne County, Miss. Recorded
4th March, 1881, 4:20 P. M.

Book WW
p. 375. Nov. 1882. Deed between Charles W. Whitaker, Guardian of John T. Harper,
Henry F. Harper, Edwin L. Harper and Charles S. Harper, wards of County of Claiborne,
Miss., of 1st part and Martha J. Whitaker, of same of 2nd part. Witnesseth: that
whereas a Term of Chancery Court of said County begun and held at Court House
thereof on Second Monday in July, 1882, it was decreed by the Court that party
of the first part should sell certain lands, etc. Witness my signature, this   day of
January, 1883. Signed C. W. Whitaker, Guardian. State of Miss., County of Claiborne;
Personally appeared before me the undersigned Clerk of Chancery Court in and for
the said County, the within named Charles W. Whitaker, Guardian of the persons
and estates of John T. Harper, Henry F. Harper, Erwin L. Harper, and Charles S. Harper,
wards, who acknowledged that he signed and delivered the foregoing instrument on
the day and year mentioned. Given under my hand and seal this 1st day of January,
A. D. 1883. A, K, Jones, Clk. Recorded 10 Jany. 1883. (Note. John T. Harper, later,
dropped the "T" for Thomas and begun using "J" for Jackson, thus making his name
John Jackson Harper, the same as his deceased father.)

p. 169. 24 June, 1890. John J. Harper, for $75. 00 to him in hand paid, released and
quit claims to Martha J. Whittaker, his interest in all the following lands, to wit:
All of Sections 20 and 22; part of Sec. 24, in T13, R3E; Sect 51, lots 2 and 3; all Sec.
52, except the West Half of West Half; 4 acres in 41; all of 53; lots 2 and 3 in 54;
lots 6, 7, 8 and 9 in 55; North onehalf of Sec. 16, T13, R4E, together with all tenements. This conveyance is intended to convey all the right, title and interest of
the said John J. Harper in and to all and any part and portion of any lands in said
County and State to which he had any right or title as an heir at law of said John
J. Harper and the said Olive B. Harper. Signed. Wit: C. R. Byrnes, Mrs. C. R. Byrnes.
Ack. by John H. Harper, 15 Jany. 1891 before A. K. Jones, Clk. Recorded Jany. 15, 1891,
2; 30 P. M. A. K. Jones, Clk.

Minutes of the Orphans Court

Book A
p. 1. Nov. 12, 1803. Met at house of Mr. William Thompson, at time and place
appointed. Present Sam'l. Bridges and Jesse Griffing, Esqs. and there not being
a sufficient number of Justices present to constitute a court, adjourned to meet
at home of Peter A. Vandorn, Esq. within an hour and accordingly a sufficient
number of Justices appeared and took their seats, to wit: Samuel Bridges, James
Harman, Waterman Crane, Jesse Griffing, Esquires. Wm. B. Elam, register of the
Orphans Court took oath.

p. 2. Will of Joseph Box produced, etc.

p. 3. Deborah Hartley, by atty., petitioned for letters of administration on estate
of John Hartley, Jr., dec'd. Granted with Stephen Bullock and Jesse Hamilton
securities. Geo. W. Humphreys, Hezekiah Harman and Elisha Flowers appointed
appraisers.

p. 6. (on. d.) Ordered that Waterman Crane, William Smith and Francis Nailer be
appointed appraisers of estate of William Thompson, dec'd., and return inventory
and appraisement in three months. (much data on this)

p. 9. Jany. 14, 1804. Letters of admr. on estate of Richard Goodin(Goodwin), dec'd.,
granted Arthur Paterson at the last December term revoked and same granted to
Phebe Goodin. Bond signed by Wm. Lindsay. Ordered: Francis Nailer and Wm. Smith
be appointed appraisers of slaves and personal estate.

34

Claiborne County
Minutes of the Orphans Court
Feb. Term 1804

p.12. Jury: Dempsey White, Llewellen Price, Ezra Marble, James McElwee, Sam'l.
Lum, Peter Lyon, Geo. W. Humphreys, James Gibson, Andrew Mundell, David Christian,
Alexr. Armstrong and Jeremiah Miller.

p.14. Letters of administration on estate of Wm. Moore to be given William Smith,
he having taken the necessary oath and gave bond with sufficient security.
John Ellison appt. Guardian of Joseph Moore, bond $1000. Waterman Crane and
G. W. Humphreys securities.

p.15. Nannett Harrington applies for letter of guardianship on estate and person
of Elizabeth Louisiana Carney, infant daughter of Arthur Carney, dec'd., as
grandmother to the child. Matilda Carney and Tobias Brashears make application
for same. Wm. Brocus, Sr., the great grandfather of the child makes application
also. // p.16. Guardianship granted Wm. Brocus, Sr.

p.20   May 29, 1804
Ordered that Nannette Brashears and Wm. Brocus, Sr., be appointed guardians of
Betsy (Elizabeth) and Thos. Calvit Harrington, minors.

p.22. Wm. Smith appt. guardian of Ann Moore and John Moore, orphans of Wm.
Moore, dec'd. $600 bond with security to be approved.

p.45. James Moore, son and heir of William Moore, dec'd., above the age of 14,
made choice of William Smith for his guardian, with Isaac Rapale and Wm. Brocus, Jr.
as security: $400.

p.69. Citation ordered to Wm. Smith to make accounting of estate of Wm. Moore
and as guardian of Ann and John Moore.

                                 August 15, 1809
p.119. On application of Penny Jones, late Penny Smith, widow of John Smith, it
is ordered that Thos. White, Stephen B. Minor, Benj. Shields and others lay off her
land.

p.127. On application of Sarah Thompson, admx. of Will Thompson, dec'd., same
order.

                                 August 13, 1810
    Andrew Mundell, of of the Commissioners appointed to run and mark roads,
from Peter Lyons to Mrs. Brashears on Big Black and make report.

    Elipt Traven and Co. versus David Christian. Stay execution until July 1st,
next.

    Ordered that Gadi Gibson oversee road from Widow Thompson's branch to
Robt. Cochran Gin and have the hands of Crane, Christian, Scotts, William Smith,
David Smith, and Robert Cochran, including own hands.

                                 February 11, 1813
p.50. Ordered that Letters of Administration be granted to Sarah Throckmorton
on the personal estate of Robert Throckmorton, dec'd., she having taken oath,
entered into bond in the sum of $1000 with John Dennis and Spencer Adams her
securities. Ordered that Ignatius Flowers, John Robertson and Wm Williams be
appraisers of said estate.

                                 November 8, 1813
p.58. Ordered that account of sales of personal estate of Robt. Throckmorton,
dec'd., returned by Isaac Powers, administrator in right of his wife, of said dec'd.,
be received and recorded. // p.70. 8 Aug. 1814. Ord. that the statements and
exhibits of the Admr and Admx, of R. L. Throckmorton, dec'd., of the insolvency
of the personal estate of sd deceased be received and recorded. Henry G. Johnson,
John Robertson and Ignatius Flowers to receive and report the Next Feb. Term of
this Court.

8th August, 1814.
Ordered that the statement and exhibits of the Admr. and Admx. of R. L. Throck-
morton, dec'd., of the insolvency of the personal estate of the said deceased be
rec'd. and recorded. Ordered that John Robertson, Henry G. Johnson and Ignatius
Flowers be Commissioners to receive and report to next February Term of this
Court on claims against the estate of R. L. Throckmorton, dec'd.

March 24, 1834
Bond of John H. Thomson, as admr. of estate of John Thomson, dec'd., $25,000.
Bondsmen: Benj. Hughes, Hugh Watt. B. Hughes declining to act as executor of the
last will and testament of John Thomson, dec'd., signed in open court.

Admr. Bonds, 1834-1840.
p. 70. Bond of Richard J. Bland, guardian of Susan Bland and Richard J. Clarke,
minor heirs to estate of Elijah Bland.

p. 72. Bond of Seth Rundell, guardian of Matilda Marble, Claiborne Co., (no parent
given) signed by Simon Rundell, W. A. Denny, Mch. 24, 1835.

p. 102. Jane M. King and Alexander Montgomery, admrs. of Wm. King, dec'd.,
Bondsmen: Chas. G. Lee and P. Briscoe, $60,000, July 27, 1835.

p. 172. Wm. D. Bush and Emily Thompson, admrs. estate of Jeremiah Thompson.
Bondsmen: Jno. Murphree, N. McDougal. Oct. 25, 1836.

Nov. 29, 1837. John K. Bush died intestate. Letters of admr. to Wm. D. Bush.

Nov. 28, 1836. Ezra Rundell, guardian of John Marble, minor under 21, son and
heir of D. Marble.

Nov. 28, 1836. James H. Maury, of Claiborne Co., appointed guardian of Elizabeth
Maury, infant dau. under 14 of James H. Maury, heir of M. F. Brashears, dec'd., bond,
$4000.

Jany. 23, 1837. Owens Dorsey, having died intestate, Wm. C. Dorsey granted letters
Administration. Bond, $15,000, signed by Eli West, R. J. Bland, John H. Thomson.
Order to sell one half of a tract on Big Black, between lands of Stampley and
W. H. Hamer, T14, R4E.

Nov. 29, 1837. W. D. Bush, admr. of John K. Bush, Elijah L. Clarke bondsman.

Jany. 23; 1838. Wm. Eggleston and Richard T. Archer, guardians of Edward B. Archer,
infant heir of Stephen C. Archer, dec'd., bond, $30,000. The same admrs. of
Stephen C. Archer, $120,000.

June 25, 1838. Mary Richey and Champ Terry admrs of John Richey, dec'd.

June 28, 1839. Wm. D. Bush, guardian of Jeremiah Washington and Josephine
Thompson, of Claiborne Co., $10,000. W. F. Dillan and R. R. Sharkey, bondsmen.

May 27, 1839. Estate of Ezra Marble, Alexander H. Horner appointed admr. and
guardian of Frances H. Marble, dau. and heir.

July 27, 1840. John Wetherall died intestate. Celia Ann Wetherall granted letters
of admr., with James Derrah.

Letters and Administrations
Jany. 24, 1842. Estate of John Wetherall. Letters of admr. granted Amariah Rollins.

Jany. 27, 1842. Franklin H. Dorsey, of Claiborne Co., apptd. guardian of Louisa
Carolina Applegate, minor under 14 years, heir of Geo. T. Applegate. Bond $2500.

Feb. 27, 1837. Wm. D. Bush and Wm. Briscoe, admrs. estate of Jeremiah Thomson,
$8,000. Land to be sold, Lots 1 and 2, Sec. 21, T13, R2E

Claiborne County
Minutes of the Orphans Court
Letters and Administrations.

Oct. 23, 1843. Horace Broughton, dec'd,, late of Claiborne County, died intestate. Nicholas Spurgin granted letters of administration.

Aug. 22, 1842. Benj. Hughes died intestate. B. W. Moreland granted letters of admr.

Dec. 4, 1843. Guardianship of Samuel Hughes, minor under 21, son and heir of Sam'l. Hughes, dec'd., to Samuel McClellan, Dec. 25, 1843. Estate of Samuel Hughes, letters granted to Samuel McClellan.

Dec. 20, 1848. Estate of Geo. W. Humphreys, letters granted to David G. Humphreys and Benj. G. Humphreys. Bond $15,000. Sec. Abram Bridges, Henry Shaifer, Jno. Humphreys.

Mch. 25, 1844. Estate of Sam'l. Hughes, letters granted Wm. Clarke and Samuel McClellan.

Oct. 28, 1844. W. B. Bush died intestate. B. W. Moreland gr. letters of admr. Lucinda M. Bush, guardian of Jeremiah M. and Emily J. Thomson, $25,000. Richard Valentine Sec.

May 2, 1844. Samuel Dalton, dec'd., late of Claiborne Co., departed this life. Goods, etc., within said state. Elijah Mount apptd admr. // May 29, 1844. Samuel Dalton estate. Wm. R. Buck granted letters of admr. (Wm. Buck was the step-father of Samuel Dalton, having married his mother, Maria, after her separation from his father, Ewell Dalton. She was her son's only surviving heir and distributee.)

Jany. 27, 1845. Lemuel N. Baldwin, of Claiborne Co., appointed guardian of Louisa Carolina Applegate, minor under 14 years, heir of George Applegate, $2500 bond.

May 26, 1845. Franklin H. Dorsey died intestate. Letters of admr. granted to George Henderson.

June 22, 1845. Trussy Bethea, of Claiborne Co., guardian, bond $1000, of Philip H. Bethea.

March Term, 1851. Citation to Martha Humphreys, widow of David S. Humphreys and guardian of her children, Elizabeth, Sampson and Agnes Humphreys, infants at law, to appear and show final acct., presented by Elias Bridgers and David D. Irwin, exrs. of the last will of Wm. Bridgers, dec'd., who was admr of estate of said David S. Humphreys.

WILLS

Book 1.

p. 11 Tobias Gibson: To Rhody Gibson a saddle horse; to three nephews: Nathaniel, son of Nath'l, dec'd., Tobias, son of Mollicy Gibson, dec'd.,; Jordan, son of Stephen Gibson. Wit: Shelley Boothe, Joseph Ferguson, Seth Caston.

p. 69. Will of Andrew Mundell: to beloved wife, Polly, my desire that she have care of son, Joseph and dau., Frances Mundell and the property that is secured to them by their uncle, Stephen Minor, dec'd., until they come of age. to Abijah, negro Randall, ten-cows and three calves, one horse, branded A. D., one dun mare, $200 and my rifle. If he dies before of age, this to go to wife Polly. To Joseph, one family Bible in two vols. and my fowling piece. To Frances, one Bible, one set of spoons. Wit: Geo. W. Humphreys, James Crane, D. G. Humphreys. (Polly, his wife, was the daughter of David Smith and his first wife, Margaret Terry.)

p. 103. Will of Stephen B. Minor. July 7th, 1821. To wife, Ann, all estate. Exrs. Joseph Moore, John Gibson.

Book A

p.79. Samuel Gibson's Will. 24th Nov.1817. No probate date given. To dau.,
Rebecca Gibson and her heirs Lot 2 of Square One of "Gibson's Port", and certain
negroes, named. To wife, Rebecca all my estate both real and personal not herein-
before.disposed of. At her d-ath, property to be sold by exrs. and proceeds invested in Bank Stock and divided as follows: To son, John Gibson, dau. Nancy Minor
and daughter Rebecca, each one-sixth; to Robt. Frazer Moore, my grandson, one-
sixth; to children of my daughter, Nancy Trimble, one-sixth, to be equally divided between them as they reach the age of 21 years or marry; td children of
daughter, Elizabeth Neely, one-sixth, to be equally divided between them as they
reach the age of 21 years or marry. To daughter, Rebecca $1500 to equalize her
portion with the rest of my children. To son, John Gibson, certain negroes, named.
To Dr. Joseph Moore, certain negroes, named. Executors have power to sell lots and
and make disposition of the estate, etc. Exrs: Son, John Gibson, Dr. Jos. Moore and
William King. Witnesses: Ann Coburn, David Downing and J.G. Clark.

p.216. Ann Gibson's Will. Sept.11,1827. To granddaughters: Martha Mellers and
Ann Gentry: to grandson William Hitch Gentry; and to dau., Rody Gentry. (Others
named but not connected.)

p.225. Feb.12,1831. Will of Abijah H. Mundell. To brother, Alfred D.S. Dillingham
and my two sisters, Frances Barnes and Margaret E. Swanson, $10.00 each. Balance
of property to my beloved wife, Ursula. Exr: Benj G. Humphreys. Wit: John A. Barnes,
Abram B. Bridgers, Harrison Liggets.

p.416. John Thomson's last will and testament. All my personal property to be
kept on the farm where, at this time, I reside, consisting of nineteen negroes,
(named), the stock of cattle, work oxen and horses, until my just debts are all
paid. After mydebts are paid, I give my beloved daughter, Myra Thomson, four
negroes, (named); To my beloved daughter, Sophia Thomson, two negroes, (named),
to my beloved daughter, Cynthia Thomson, two negroes, (named); to my beloved son,
John Higgason Thomson, a negro man, (named), to my beloved son, Alfred Todd
Thomson, one negro man, (named). When the property is divided among the heirs
equally, if the heirs cannot divide them, they shall not be drawn for but valued
and charged to each heir according to valuation. To my before-named children,
the tract I live on, 572 acres, fraction Sec. No.3, T13. R1E, and the tract on the
lower side, about 111 acres, to be sold at public sale on one, two or three yrs. credit
and the money equally divided amongst the heirs. The tract in Concordia, La,,
opposite to where I now live and now in suit with Stephen Douglass, when suit is
decided, if in my favour, the land shall be sold and one half of the net price shall
be given to Robt. McCay, of Hinds County, and the other half divided amongst the
before-mentioned heirs. To my beloved daughter, Nancy Dillingham, for divers
good causes, I do give her $50 when my property is divided. As A.D.S. Dillingham
owes me considerable money, and if he will settle with my executors, for what I have
paid for the firm of Dillingham and Thomson, then my daughter will be entitled to
an equal share of my property,, after deducting the price of a negro woman I gave
her when she married. I appoint Robert McCay, Benj. Hughes and John Higgason
Thomson as exrs., 30 March, 1833. Wit: Brooke Hill, Dennis Burns, Geo. P. Applegate.
(Written and signed by testator). (A.D.S. Dillingham died of cholera in June 1833)

p.149. Will of Waterman Crane, Feb. 5, 1826. Wife: Catherine. Legatees: Wm. Crane
and Robt. Mitchell, grandsons: James Crane, son, Carolina Christian and Catherine
Quinn, granddaughters: Lucy McNeil and Clarissa Young, daughters. Exrs: Wife,
James Crane and William Young. (Waterman Crane, one of the earliest settlers of
Claiborne County, from Halifax, Nova Scotia; married Catherine Brashears. Goodspeed
Vol. I, p. 602.)

Book A.

p.304. Nuncupative will of Thelemiah Rhodes. Clothes and money, after debts are
paid, to mother, Nancy Biggs, of Cuba, Clinton Co., Ohio. She has six children by last
marriage. I have no full brothers or sisters. Feb.2, 1855.

Book B.

p.6. July 12, 1838. Will of Lewis T. Grubbs. All property to be sold except horse
and saddle and one bed, which I will to Levi E. Beard. From proceeds of sale to
wife, Pyrena Grubbs, $12,000; to Levi E. Beard $500; to brother, Thos. Grubbs,
$25,000. The rest equally divided between my brothers, John F. and Thurston Grubbs,
and sisters, Mary Colley, Eliz. Hallaway and Nancy Duncan. Exrs: Isaac Powers and
Horace M. Booth. Wit: Wm. Jones, H. M. Booth, Carter Wood. Prob. July 23, 1838.

p.65. Nov.4, 1844. Will of Mary Barnes. Property to children and grand-children.
To grandson, Albert T. Bridgers, son Elias Bridgers, gr-dau. Emily McIntyre, Mary
Bridgers, dau. of Sampson Bridgers; to Martha Humphreys; to grandson Sam'l.
Bridgers; to Thos. McLaughlin, Benj. G. Humphreys, Mary E. D. Humphreys and Thos.
Barnes, each one dollar. Sons: Wm., Elias, and Abram. Son, Wm. exr. Wit: Geo.
W. Humphreys, Stephen Humphreys. Prob. May 26, 1845.

p.70. Will of Ann S. Singleton, Oct.17, 1844. Wit: Milford Hunter, R. C. Hawkins.
Prob. Sept. 1845.

p.100. Will of Mary C. Archer, of Cumberland Co., Va., to son, Richard T. Archer,
of Miss., property from brother, James P. Cocke, of Amelia Co., Va. To grandson,
Stephen Edward Archer, only surviving son of my son, Stephen C. Archer, when
he becomes 21. Jan. 27, 1842. (signed) Mary C. Archer. Wit: Dan'l. A. Wilson, James
Hobson, James S. Archer. Codocil, Apr. 29, 1844. Mch. 8, 1845. Probated Feb. 26,
1849 in Cumberland Co., Va.

p.109. 26 Apr. 1846. Will of Abram B. Bridgers, sound mind, equal division among
children; Edward, Alfred, Mary, George, Margaret and Sampson. Wm. Bridgers and
Benj. G. Humphreys exrs.

p.107. May 2, 1849-Aug. 29, 1849. Will of Amos Burnet. Brother John and his
children; brother Wm. D. Burnet and children; sister Laura Burnett and her children;
Sister Ann Gibson, formerly Ann Burnett. My undivided one-fifth interest in slaves
to brothers and sisters, John, Wm. D., Ann and Laura. Undivided one-sixth as one of
of six children of my father, John Burnet, Sr.

p.130. Peter Hedrick's will, 20th July 1849; proved 24th October, 1820. Farmer.
Pay all debts, of which there are few, punctually. To son, Benjamin F. Hedrick,
a horse, saddle and bridle, two cows and calves and three sheep. Grandson, Thomas
J. Segrest, two hundred dollars on twenty-first birthday, but to be returned to estate
if he dies before. Beloved wife, Susannah Hedrick, all rest and residue of real and
personal estate; at her death to be divided between children, Mary Davis, John A.
Hedrick, Caroline W. Bailey and Benjamine F. Hedrick. Exrs. son-in-law, Josea Davis
and son, John A. Hedrick. Signed: Peter Hedrick. Wit: Jackson Dunbar, John D. Goza,
Henry J. Wilson.

p.245. June 27, 1857. Will of Mrs. Ruth D. Humphreys. To son, Samuel Cobun
Humphreys, all my estate. In event of his death before 21 years my sister Balissa
shall have all negroes given by my father, Joseph Davenport, at the time or shortly
after my marriage.; D. G. Humphreys to have plantation and landed estate and
negroes belonging to it. Wit: M. McGill. H. McAlpine. W. P. Holloway. Mch. 25, 1857.

p.403. Will of James Maury, Feb. 18, 1871. Son, James F. Maury, law library and misc.
books of every description. Wife, Lucinda, dwelling in Port Gibson, lots and three
store houses. Wit: Ben. F. Chisholm, Chas S. Mason, Fred F. Myles. Jany 3, 1874.

Book B

p. 22. Will of Peter Hickman, formerly of Virginia but at this time of Claiborne
Co., Miss. Debt to be paid first to John Saunders, which amounts to about $1000,
but I'll leave that to him and trust his honesty. I wish, if my family move that
Saunders will move, too, and help my wife take care of her children and I hope
that they live harmoniously together. Property in Va. and Tenn. to be sold at best
mark. Exrs. for that sale, Harrison Hickman and Jacob Merchant ; exrs for Miss.
property, friend, James E. P. Bacon. Spare no pains in collecting debt owed. (n. d.)

p. 261. Martha Archer Conger's will. June 11, 1853. All debts against me and
estate of my father and brother to be paid. Personal property to friend and lawyer,
William Sidney Wilson. Miss Mary C. Thompson to remain at Eildon, and Mr. Franklin
T. Thompson, who resides with me, after salary paid, to receive one-third of cattle
and hogs and my father's gun. Rev. Zebulon Butler, one negro. (Wm. Wilson deposes
that on Sept. 8, 1857, Mrs. Martha Archer Tucker, formerly Martha A. Conger died
in Miss. but domiciled in Parish of Carroll, La., left will, dated June 11, 1843.
Tighlman Tucker acquainted with Martha Conger and knows her handwriting.
Silas M. Tucker deposes the same.)

p. 399. Will of Jane M. Neely, 10 May, 1781. Filed Sept. 2, 1873. Rec. same day by
Solomon Unger, Clk. Jane M. Neely, of Claiborne Co., Miss. To my grandchildren,
Ann L. Stacy, Mary Stacy, John Stacy, Clara K. Stacy, the legacy left me by their
father, David S. Stacy, late of Concordia Parish, La. To Clara S. Stacy and her
heirs the set of silverware presented to me by her father. To my daughter, Clara
Snyder, for the use of her and her father, all the balance of my silverware and
my household goods, horses, oxen, sheep and farming utensils, except hereinafter
bequeathed to Wm. A. King. And after the death of John G. Neely said property to
belong to sd Clara Snyder. To my son, Wm. A. King, '400 acres known as Cox Tract
in Claiborne Co, To my grand-children, Kate and Bertha Crane and their heirs my
town lots in Port Gibson, Miss. My son, Wm. A. King, my daughter, Clara Snyder
and my husband, John G. Neely, share and share alike the proceeds of the sales
and rents of my property in Mississippi City. The residue of my property, real
and personal and mixed to my grand-children, the children of David S. Stacy, dec'd.,
of Robt. King, dec'd., and Robert Crane, dec'd. My husband, John G. Neely and my
dau., Clara Snyder, exor and extx, no bond required. Dated Buckhorn Plantation,
Claiborne Co., Miss. 10 May 1871. Wit: Reeve Lewis, Frank A. Jones, Olivia Jones.
Filed Sept. 2, 1873 by Solomon Unger, Clk.

p. 407. Will of Catherine S. Prince, dated .... 1854. Filed 25 Sept. 1860. To my
grandson, Bayliss Earl Prince, a negro boy named Thompson; to my grandson, Bayliss
Earl Humphreys, a negro boy named Horace; to my grand-daughter, Catherine Prince
Humphreys, a negro girl Amanda. All the rest of my estate, real and personal,
after payment of my debts and above legacies to my daughter, Catherine B. Humphreys
and to the children of my deceased son William B. Prince; one-half to my said
daughter and the other half to the children of my son William. Exer: my brother,
Nathaniel Jeffries. Signed. Wit: Wm. Hughes, James Jeffries, Edward Coleman.
Codocils: To my grandson, Bayliss Earl Humphreys, my servant boy, Isaac, in place
of the one I willed him several years ago, who has since died, his name being
Horace. I also will that my servant man, Green, at my death go to my son's
children at his appraised value as they own his family. I will that my daughter,
C. Bayliss Humphreys shall take the servants I heired from my mother's estate
as a portion of her half of my negro property, they having relations living in
the neighborhood desire that she should take them. (Names given) Also I desire
that my furniture be equally divided between my daughter, C. Bayliss Humphreys
and my daughter-in-law, Martha Prince and that they should divide it themselves.
I want my daughter, Bayliss to inherit five thousand dollars more than my son's
children because she has had more trouble with me. July 4, 1860. Filed July 23,
1860. James A. Gagem Clk. by Ben F. Booth, D. C.

Book B.

p. 362. Will of Elizabeth H. Shaifer, 22 April 1867, probated Dec. 24, 1867.
All my just debts to be paid by my executor as soon as possible. I will to my
son, Abram Shaifer's wife, Amanda C. Shaifer, and her children that she may have
by my son A. K. Shaifer; and Ben Humphreys Shaifer and Adam Keller Shaifer, the
children by his, A. K. Shaifer's former wife, Elizabeth Shaifer, all my personal
property and estate of whatsoever and all my monies and causes in action and
effect. My son to be executor with no bond required by Probate Court. Signed
E. H. Shaifer. Wit: Maria Buck, Benj. G. Humphreys, Caroline Buck. Probated and
admitted to record Dec. 24, 1867. Jas. A. Maxwell, Judge of Probate. Opened and
filed for record, 23rd Dec. 1867 and this 20th Dec. truly recorded. Jas. A. Gage, Clk.
per Jno. R. Gage, D. C.

Book 4.

p. 284. Isaac Powers' will of (Rocky Springs), Claiborne Co., Miss., 28th December,
1853, proved 28th Fenruary 1859, before J. A. Maxwell, Judge of Probate. First, to
son Henry G. J. Powers all my lands in Hinds County, Miss., lying on waters of Five
Mile Creek, 560 acres (described); also all that part of Lot one adjoining Hardwood
Jones and Henry's plantation, and the privilege, after my decease of paying my
estate same amount I paid C. B. Clark for Ferry Place, thereby becoming its owner,
also certain negroes (named), together with all horses, cattle, hogs, farmer's tools,
household and kitchen furniture I have heretofore advanced him. My son, Felix A.
Powers has received his portion of land estate in plantation he sold to Richard
Harding, also I have given son Felix certain negroes, (named) together with $1200
paid to said Felix by me at sundry times, also all horses, cattle, hogs, farming utensils,
household and furniture advanced to him heretofore. To grand-daughter, Delia A.
Powers, certain negroes, (named). To grand-daughter, Cora Powers certain negroes,
(named). To my son, W. B. Powers my lands on Big Sandy Creek in Claiborne Co., Miss.
(described), and to said son certain negroes (named) and the horses, cattle, hogs,
farming utensils, household and kitchen furniture advanced to him heretofore. To
my son, John R. Powers my home plantation land on waters of Little Sandy Creek in
Claiborne Co., 600 acres (description), also certain negroes, (named) and all horses,
cattle, hogs, farming utensils, household and kitchen furniture heretofore advanced
to him. To my step-son, L. R. Throckmorton, during his natural life the use of the
boy named Cyrus; also give and forgive unto said Throckmorton the sum of four
hundred dollars advanced for which I hold his receipt; the negro man Cyrus to
return to my estate at said Throckmorton's decease. I also will and desire that
all my estate of whatsoever kind now in hands of my wife remain in her possession
for her use and benefit during her natural life, after her decease all real and personal estate not given or bequeathed may be divided or sold and distributed
equally among my heirs. Executors: my son, Henry G. J. Powers, sole executor, without
bond. Signed Isaac Powers. Wit: A. E. Thomas, D. R. Porter and Geo. P. McLean. (L. R.
Throckmorton was son of Mordecai Throckmorton and wife, Sarah Burney, of
Jefferson Co., Miss. Isaac Powers was her second husband.)

David George Humphreys and Mary Coburn. Jacob Rickhorn surety. Dec. 20, 1816.
Married Dec. 22 by J. Rickhorn, M. G.

Abraham Shaifer and Elizabeth Humphreys. David Downing surety. May 13, 1817.

Samuel Smith, of Choctaw Agency, and Mary Osborn. Joseph Moore surety. May 11, 1817.

Wm. Conger and Rachel Thompson, March 18, 1817.

Jesse Alford and Peggy Fife. Thos. W. Cogan surety, July 8, 1817.

Richard Dorsey and Phoebe Armstrong, Alexander Armstrong surety. Apr. 28, 1818.

Joseph Beiller and Margaret Mackey. Thos. W. Cogan surety. March 16, 1818.

Thomas Dawson and Patsy Brooks. William Brooks surety. Oct. 26, 1818.

Robert Thompson and Rebecca Jones. Jonathan Ballou surety. Jany. 19, 1820.

Alfred D. S. Dillingham and Nancy Thomson. Consent of John Thomson. Tobias
Gibson surety. Married by A. K. Shaifer, J. P. June 20, 1820.

John Gibson and Martha Lindsay.

David Gibson and Mary Mundell. C. Haring surety. May 1, 1820. Married by A. K.
Shaifer, J. P.

Ira D. Walton and Jane Bland. Copeland McKee surety. June 11, 1822.

John Hartley and Harriet Charkey. John Bivins, surety. Feb. 8, 1822.

John Bivins and Christiana Hartley. W. A. Cash, surety. Feb. 20, 1822.

Jacob E. Stampley and Mary Flower. Josiah Flower, surety. Mch. 27, 1823.

Garrett Keirn and Lucy Leake. John Esty surety. Dec. 25, 1823 by Randall Gibson.

William Thomson and Hannah Ballow. Joshua Ballow, surety. July 28, 1824.

John S. King and Hulda Flowers. Randall Gibson, surety. June 10, 1824.

Dorsey Bates and Nancy Sargent. J. W. King, surety. Aug. 13, 1822.

David D. Gibson and Catherine Knowland. John Bettis, surety. Sept. 4, 1822.

Archibald MCEvers and Catherine Alford. Peleg Spencer, surety. Sept. 1, 1824.

Eliphalet Roane and Polly Gibson. Amos Whiting, surety. Aug. 28, 1824.

John T. Dorsey and Ann E. Hoite. Geo. Applegate surety. May 25, 1825.

Jeremiah Thomson and Emily Bullock. Thomson Strother, surety. Oct. 11, 1825.

Nugent Perry and Louisa Dorsey. Geo. P. Applegate, surety, Nov. 11, 1825.

Geo. P. Applegate and Eliza Dorsey. John T. Dorsey, surety. 28 July, 1825. Married
by Randall Gibson.

John Valentine and Elizabeth Roberts. Wm. Rowland, surety. June 10, 1826. Married
by Wm. Liles, J. P.

Thompson Strother and Elizabeth Marble. Wm. H. White, surety. Jan. 25, 1827.

Stephen L. Smith and Druscilla Marble. Reuben Jones, surety. Feb. 1, 1827.

Walter Strother and Harriet Hartley. Allen B. Bridgers, surety. Mch. 15, 1827.

Richard Stampley and Abigail Smith. Benj. Lewis. surety. Aug. 16, 1827.

Abijah H. Mundell and Ursula Ann Stampley. Dennis Burns, surety. Nov. 16, 1830.

Edward Swanson and Margaret E. Dillingham. Jno. M. Maury, surety. Dec. 23, 1828.

Thompson Strother and Mary L. Yeiser. Benj. Strother and George W. Yeiser, surety. Oct. 23, 1833.

Albert M. Sessions and Lucretia R. Kercheval. June 11, 1834.

Samuel Rusk and Myra Thomson. Wm. T. Fisher, surety. Oct. 1, 1834.
Edward Newell and Celia Dorsey. Frank W. Turpin, surety. Sept. 25, 1834.

Francis B. Ragland and Mrs. Ursula Mundell. Thos. M. Newell, surety. May 10, 1826. (She was the widow of Abijah H. Mundell and the daughter of David Stampley of Jefferson Co., Miss.)

Owings Dorsey and Mary Ann Scott. Edward Dorsey, surety. June 13, 1836.
Benonie Taylor and Hannah Thompson. W. M. Hall, surety. July 27, 1836.

Lemuel Gustine and Sophia Thomson. Wm. M. Willoughby surety. Jany. 31, 1838. Married by R. H. Ramsey, minister of the P. E. Church, Diocese of Mississippi.

John C. Johnson and Margaret S. Shaifer. G. R. Girault surety. July 17, 1850. (She was named for her mother's grandmother, Margaret Terry Smith, wife of David Smith, and in one record is called Margaret Smith Shaifer.)

Everard M. Eggleston and Mrs. Harriet B. Sayer. E. Archer, surety. Apr. 4, 1857.
William L. Rusk and Mrs. Louise Nugent. Richard J. Bland, surety. Apr. 4, 1834. (She was a Dorsey)

John Wetherall and Celia Ann Strother. Richard Bland, surety. 15 Feb. 1838.

Thos. J. Thomas and Mary B. Chunn. John S. Bradshaw, surety. 27 Sept. 1837.

Samuel H. Butler and Mary Ann Thompson, 25 Oct. 1837.

Philip Bethea and Missouri Buchanan. Martin O. Hopkins, surety. 13 Aug. 1839.
W. P. Lowry and Celia Ann Wetherall. Trussy Bethea, surety. Oct. 26, 1842.
Franklin H. Dorsey and Martha Ann Henderson. Thos. W. Broughton, surety. May 17, 1843.

Edward H. Dorsey and Rachel A. Henderson. Daniel McDougal surety. 18 Jan. 1843.
Thos. W. Broughton and Martha L. Dorsey. Nath'l. P. Moody, surety. May 12, 1845.
Stephen P. Shaifer and Esther W. Patton. Nath'l. P. Moody, surety. Nov. 1845.
Sam'l. R. Bertron and Catherine M. Barnes. Josiah Foster, surety. May 31, 1847.
Trussy Bethea and Malinda Ingram. Thos. B. Howard, surety. Oct. 14, 1847.
Peyton E. Moore and Louisa Carolina Applegate. W. McDougall, surety. 18 Nov. 1847.

Abram Green and Carolina Maury. Robt. F. Moore, surety. Feb. 15, 1849.
Wm. A. Lum and Lucretia M. Ervin. James E. Boyce, surety. Married by Thos. Owens. Consent of step-father, Elijah L. Clarke, stating her mother also consents, 5 Jan. 1846.

Reese M. Broughton and Eliz. Ann Calhoun. W. T. Owen, surety. 25 July 1850.
Wm. Hughes and Mary Bertron. Joseph M. Magruder surety. 31 May, 1847.
Samuel P. Duncan and Martha R. Parker, James H. Maury, surety. 9 May, 1854.
Chas. I. Purnell to Clara Bertron. Henry Hughes, surety. 25 May 1857.

Book A

p. 13. Oct. 28, 1809. James Thompson to Henry D. Downs, for $1100, 340 acres on the Miss. River about 12 miles below Walnut Hills, which James Thompson purchased at public sale. Signed. Wit: Cassandra Shipp, Bartlet (x) Shipp.

p. 20. Oct. 28, 1809. Henry Downs, admr. of estate of William Downs, dec'd. Wit: Archd. Greve, Bartlett Shipp.

p. 24. April 3, 1805. Rebecca Gibson, gift deed to her children, at her death, 2/3 of her slaves. //p. 27. Same date, Rebecca Gibson, to her sister, Honor Darby, the balance of her estate. Wit: Shelby Booth, Henry Middleton.

p. 56. Mch. 11, 1813. Green G. Clayton, of Warren Co., Miss. Ter., Lot No. 19 in Warrenton, adj. lot of John G. Jones and James Nolen. //p. 61. Mch. 13, 1813. Wm. Thompson, of Hamilton Co., Ohio, to James Scarlett, of Warren Co., for $94, Lot 19 in Warrenton. Signed. Wit: John W. Powell, Thos. Dewitt. // p. 63 Mch. 13. 1813. James Scarlett, of Warren Co., to Wm. Thompson, of Hamilton Co., Ohio, for $100, Lot 34 in Warrenton. Same witnesses

p. 129. Oct. 7, 1818. Gideon Gibson, of Warren Co., gives power of atty. to Chesley Daniel, of Marion Dist., S. C. to sell my part of the Grove lands. Wit: H. D. Downs.

p. 176. Oct. 10, 1818. To Commissioners for dividing Claiborne and Warren Counties, from Andrew Glass, Edmund Reeves and John Hyland, partners, owning the land on which Warrenton (then County seat) is seated.

p. 197. 15 Sept. 1818. Anthony Durden to Willis B. Vick, bill of sale, for $2900, six negroeslaves, named. Ack. before James Knowland, J. P. 6th Jany. 1819.

p. 206. June 29, 1818. Deed of Gift. Jeremiah Thompson, of Warren Co., Miss., for consideration and regard, to my grandson, Jeremiah Thompson, son of my son, William Thompson, and for $1.00. a negro boy, named George, about 8 years old, one yoke of oxen and six cows and calves, marked J. T. Signed Wit: John Blanchard, Hor. G. Willis.

p. 210. 12 Feb. 1819. Indenture between Green C. Caston and Andrew Glass, both of Warren Co., for $25.00, fifteen feet of ground off Lot No. 19, in Town of Warrenton. Signed. Wit: Edmd. Reeves, B. C. Lansdell, Sam'l. F. Chisholm. Ack. by Edmund Reeves before Thos. B. Tompkins. 12 Feb. 1819.

p. 226. 5 Nov. 1818. Daniel Hickson, of Warren Co., for $2200, to John Treadwell, of same, all the goods, household stuff, books and implements of household and all other goods and chattles whatsoever now in my possession. Signed: Daniel Hickson. The sd Daniel giving and delivering to sd John Treadwell "one set of Table Spoons" in the name of the whole goods and premises, in the presence of George Downs, Samuel Treadwell. Sworn to, the 9th of May 1819 before James Knowland, J. P.

Book B.
p. 116. Mch. 13, 1822. Wm. Thomson, of Hamilton Co., Ohio, to Reuben Davis, of Warren Co., Miss., for $80, Lot 34. Wit: Elijah Pace, Thos. D. Downs, Wm. Evans.

p. 144. 26 March 1822. James Gibson and Frances, his wife, Jordan Gibson and Anthony Durden and Mary Eliza, his wife, of Warren Co., to Wm. Briscoe, for $3000, 100 acres in Warren Co,, described, which was granted by the U. S. to sd James, Jordan and Mary Elizabeth. Signed by the four.

Book C

p.45. Oct.15,1823. Murphy Bradford sells to Alfred D.S.Dillingham 540 acres o
on the Miss.River,immediatelt below John Rails, with all logs and planks and
scantlings sawed for a new house; for $1000 cash, 11 bales of cotton 1825; 11
bales of cotton,1826, allowing 12 and 1/2 cents per pound. Both parties of
Mississippi. Both signed. Wit:William Thomson.

p.72. Nov.18,1822. Andrew Glass,sheriff, to John Thomson, 110 acres from
suit of John Thomson against the land and chattles of William Strother, for $1800,
Sec.3,& 13.R1E, on which Strother lives.

p.75. Aug.23,1822. William Downs, of Claiborne Co.,Miss. Ter., to Henry D.
Downs and Joseph Downs,of same. An ordinance of the State of Georgia, for
services done as Commr. apptd by the Legislature of Ga.,Feb.21,1784, for the
purpose of examining a certain district of land on the Tennessee River and grant-
ing warrants of survey. William Downs transfers to Henry D.Downs and Joseph
Downs, for their promisory notes for $3000, sd ordinance and whatever land Georgia
may allow for said services,(signed) H.D.Downs, my right and title to within as
he has made payment out of his own funds. (signed) Jos.Downs.

p.123. Jan.7,1824. Daniel Futral,of Warren Co.,for $1800, to Wm.A.Land and
Chas.W.Land, of Warren, a negro girl, Middy, aged 14, boy,Isaac, 12;boy Burrell,
10, boy Green,6,boy Jacob, 4. Signed. Wit: J.Bland,Wm.Rushing.

Book D.

p.6. July 1,1818. Henry D.Downs, for love and affection, to daughter,Milly
Douglas Gibson, a negro woman named Betty,aged 37 years. Signed. Wit: H.A.
Downs. //p.33. July 16, 1825. Henry D.Downs, to Milly D.Downs, two negroes,
for her natural life, then to revert to him or hisr heirs. Signed: H.D.Downs.
Wit : A.C.Downs.

p.26. Mch.8,1826. James Hinson, of Vicksburg, to Rowland Thompson and A.G.
McNutt. Whereas James Hinton is largely indebted to John Thompson,Sr., who
became security for sd Hinson on several bonds and notes, for this and the sum
of $5.00 to Roland Thompson and A.G.McNutt, two lots in.Vicksburg on Grove
and Walnut Streets, now known as Steam Boat Hotel and all personal property in
said hotel. Deed of.trust. If foreclosed, proceeds To go to pay note for $1000
to John Thompson. // Bk.E.p.24. A.G.McNutt, Rowland Thompson and John
Thompson with James Hinson (same seal as above),Rowland Thompson as of
Amite County.

p.489. John Thomson, of Warren Co., to Robert and Henderson McCay, deed of
trust on 572 acres whereon Thomson now resides, for $1787 and int. payable to
Samuel Dorsey, endorsed by Robert McCay. (signed) John Thomson.

Book E.

p.66. John Thompson (Thomson), of Warren Co., Miss.,for $5,000, to Robert McCay
and Samuel Dorsey,of Claiborne Co., Frac. No.3 T13 R1E and negroes David,45,Godfrey
25, Nathan 28, Isaac 22, Isham 25, Armistead 35, Polly 17 & son, Mariah 23 & dau.
Ann 2, Beck 50,Henry 40, Lucinda 23, Nat, a cripple 40, cotton and corn crop now
growing, 6 horses, 80 cattle, 25 sheep,50 hogs, 3 yoke of oxen, furnituremetc. Wit:
R.R.Sharkey,James King, Amos Whiting. Ack.in Claiborne Co. 3rd Oct.1828 before
N.Hansfield,J.P. Recorded, Warren Co. Jany 29,1829.

p.149. 5 June 1829. William C.Cross, of Warren Co.,Miss., for $1517, to William
Pescod, of same. House and lot of land, No.52, in Town of Vicksburg, corner of
East and Cherry Sts. Signed. Wit: W.L.Sharkey, Adaline S.A.Cross,wife of Wm.
C.Cross, releases dower 1st July 1829. Cross ack. before Hartwell VickmJ.P.,
6th June 1829. Recorded July 23,1829. Cross ack.before Hartwell Vick,J.P.6th June,
1829. Recorded July 23,1829. B.Wren Clk.

Book E

p. 203. Jesse Guice, of Franklin Co., Miss., for $1500, sells to Ephraim Guice, of Concordia Parish, La., 159 88/100 acres in Warren Co. Signed. Jesse Guice. Wit: Jacob Guice, Jr., John W. Spiars. Ack. by Jesse Guice before Jonathan Rupel, Esq., J. P. of Franklin Co., Miss. 24 Mch. 1828. Recorded Oct. 25, 1829, Warren Co., by B. Wrenn, Clk.

p. 349. Feb. 18, 1830. Owings Dorsey, of Claiborne Co., to Horace Carpenter, of Port Gibson, deed of trust on slave, horses, oxen, cattle and furniture, for $800, which Dorsey owes Carpenter. Ack. by Dorsey before Samuel Hoit, J. P. 19th Feb. 1830. Claiborne Co., Miss. Recorded 29 April 1830, E. G. Cook, Clk. Warren County, Miss.

p. 430. 6 Nov. 1830. Albert G. Creath and Mary G. Creath, his wife, of Warren Co., Miss., for $900, to Josiah C. Smith, of said Co., house and lot in Town of Vicksburg, the same being the present residence of sd Albert and Mary, fronting on 2nd East Street, bounded by west corner of Lot 52, now in possession of Wm. Pescod, north by house and lot of Wm. R. Bay, now used and occupied by Bank of Discount and Deposit of State of Miss. Both signed and ack. same date before Jas. Connell, J. P., E. G. Cook, Clk. of Court.

p. 442. 24 Nov. 1830. Henry Morse and Eliza W. Morse, his wife, of Warren Co., Miss,, for $200, lots in Vicksburg to Frances Gibson and her heirs. Signed by both and acknowledged before Jas. Cornell, J. P., 24 Nov. 1830. Recorded same day by E. G. Cook, Clk.

p. 473. 10 Nov. 1830. Sarah C. Lane and John Lane, of Warren Co., Miss., for $1000, to Gideon Gibson, Lot seventy, Square 10, etc. Signed by both and ack. before Hartwell Vick, J. P. 1st Dec. 1830.

p. 493-4. 14 Feb. 1831. Edward Swanson to William R. Campbell, mortgage. Robt. Garland, trustee. Whereas, 1st Nov. 1830, Wm. R. Campbell went on bond of Edw. Swanson to Laurence Keys & Co., of N. Y., for $1025 for goods, wares, drugs and medecines; and again for $3000 to Keys; Edward Swanson mortgages all right to two quarter sections of land in Washington Co., Miss. and slaves Tom, 30, Lucy, 22, Randal, 35, Malinda, 22, Hannah, 28, Lewis, 22, and 3 ch. of Malinda. All signed and ack. 18 Feb. 1831.

Book F.

p. 26. 28 May 1831. Daniel Whitaker, surviving executor of last will and testament of Reuben Newman, dec'd., to Josiah Smith, the highest bidder at sale, for $550, all that part of said lot laid off as Newman's dower, fronting on Cherry St., 70 ft. and running back to Doctor Bay's lot. Ack. in court, 30 May, 1831.

p. 45. 5 May 1831. William Pescod, of Warren Co., to Josiah C. Smith, ten inches of ground fronting on second East St., part of Lot 52, in Vicksburg, purchased by Pescod of Wm. C. Cross, upon which the last dwelling of said Smith encroaches. Signed and ack. in court, 18 June 1831.

p. 46. June 1, 1831. Thos. Anderson, mortgages to J. C. Smith. Whereas J. C. Smith has deeded to Thos. Anderson a certain lot, Anderson mortgages to Smith to secure to him payment of $2367 and interest and $10 cash, part of Lot 52, including the residence of sd Smith and the old frame house formerly occupied by Mrs. Newman as her dower. Notes due every year. Ack. in Ct. 20 June 1831.

p. 51. June 1, 1831. J. C. Smith, of Warren Co. to Thos. Anderson, deed to the property on which Thos. Anderson mortgaged to Smith for payment in above record. Signed by J. C. Smith and ack. before W. H. Benton, J. P. June 18, 1831. Recorded 9th July 1831. E. G. Cook, Clk.

Book F.

p. 219. 16 May 1832. Thomas Sumpter to Samuel McCray, for $300, to be paid
Jany. 1. 1832, and $500 to be paid on Jany. 4, 1834, deed of trust on Lot No. 77,
Square 12 in Vicksburg. Trustee, Edwin Gray Cook. Thomas (x) Sumpter, Sam'l.
D. McCray, E. G. Cook. Endorsement on the record that contract was cancelled and
property now vests in S. D. McCray. Not dated.

p. 314. Jan. 31, 1833. Owen Dorsey and Martha L. Dorsey, his wife, of Warren Co.,
to Thos. R. Randolph, of same, 73 acres. Signed by both and ack. before Jas. Bland,
Associate Justice, same day.

p. 349. June 1, 1833. D. and F. W. Gibson sell to Thos. J. Gibson, all of Warren Co.,
for $630, sell a negro man, named Garrison, aged 25. Signed: D. & F. W. Gibson. Ack.
personally by David Gibson, Sr., one of the former. 4th June 1833.

p. 475. 3 Oct. 1833. John Thompson and Rachel F., his wife, for $213, to William
S. Bodley and John Templeton, Jr., an undivided moiety in Lot No. 307, Square 64
in Town of Vicksburg. Signed by both and ack. before Jas. Cornell, J. P. same date,
Rachel releasing her dower. Recorded 7th Dec. 1834. John A, Marsh, Clk.

p. 525. 30 Dec. 1833. William Vick, of Warren Co., Miss., for $150 paid me by Peter
Scrimshaw, admr. of estate of Owen Rhodes and $300 paid to me by said Owen Rhodes
during his lifetime, to said Peter Scrimshaw and Serena T. Rhodes, the widow and
admx. of said Owen Rhodes and to Thomas J. Rhodes and Emily Rhodes, children of
said Owen Rhodes, lots Nos. 11 and 13 in part of my tract of land below, in Warren Co.,
Miss., on the east bank of the Miss. River. Signed Wm. Vick. Ack. 30 Dec. 1833 before
J. P. Harrison, J. P. Recorded 12 Feb. 1834. John A. Marsh, Clk.

p. 550. 28 Mch. 1834. Mary E. Howard, wife of Stephen Howard, of Warren Co., Miss.,
having right and dower in 160 acres which is now, with the exception of said right
and dower, the property of George Selser, does hereby grant, remise and forever quit
claim to George Selser, his heirs, etc. all said right and dower. Signed and ack.
before James Cornell, J. P. and recorded by clerk, John A. Marsh, same day.

p. 552. 24 Feb. 1834. David Gibson & Co. to Joseph Templeton and Harris Wright &
Co., deed of trust for $1000, lot in Warrenton formerly occupied by J. B. Sharkey &
Co., for a store, then by David and F, W. Gibson, now in possession of David Gibson
& Co. Signed by David Gibson, Jr., for David Gibson, F. W. Gibson, Harris Wright,
Joseph Templeton.

Book K

p. 338. Jan. 11, 1838. Stephen Duncan, of Adams Co., releases Ambrose and Gideon
Gibson from promisory notes and contract and empowers Ambrose to cancel same
legally for him. Signed by Stephen Duncan before Ralph North, Clerk of Probate
Court, Adams. Co.; 11 January 1833.

Book Q

p. 497. William R. Campbell and Margaret, his wife, to James F. Sothoron, of Maryland,
for $300, land at Walnut Hills, in Warren Co., near Yazoo Road. Signed: Wm. R. Campbell,
and ack. by him before Miles C. Folks, Mayor of Vicksburg, 27 July 1841. Recorded
23 August, 1841 by A. H. Rowlett, Clk.

Book B

p. 82. Nov. 6, 1816. Patrick Sharkey and Martha Gibson, both of Warren Co. John Hyland, surety. Wit: H. A. Downs.

Book C.

p. 2. Sept. 8, 1818. Robert Sharkey and Sally Booker. Wm. Booker, surety.

p. 47. Sept. 16, 1816. Anthony Durden and Mary Gibson. Willis B. Vick, surety.

p. 146. Dec. 14, 1822. Allen Sharkey and Ann Maria Newman. R. Smith, surety.

p. 180. Jan. 1824. Owen Rhodes and Serena Karr. L. Spann, surety.

p. 185. Aug. 17, 1824. Tobias E. Brashears and   Thomson Strother, surety. (Girl's name not filled but she was most probably Lucinda Bullock.)

Book D

p. 109. Apr. 5, 1828. Wm. D. Bush, of Warren Co., and Mrs. Elizabeth Stephens. Henry Payne, surety. Married by John Bitner, J. P. Apr. 6th.

p. 138. Jany. 1st, 1822. George Rapale and Elizabeth Stevens. K. A. Martin, surety.

p. 139. Jany. 14, 1829. Jefferson Nailor and Eliza Gibson. Thomas Anderson, surety.

p. 140. Jany. 20, 1829. Richard Shoat and Eliza Newman. P. Sims, surety.

p. 156. May 21, 1829. Henry Blanton and Nancy Hamilton. E. G. Cook, surety. Rebecca Hamilton, gives consent that John H. Blanton marry her daughter, Nancy. James Hamilton appears before the court and swears that he heard his mother give above consent.

p. 189. March 29, 1830. Joseph Beard and Catherine Parks, John Ford, surety.

p. 274. 14 March, 1832. Wm. D. Bush and Mrs. Lucinda Brashears. Jonathan Bullock, surety.

p. 305. March 7, 1832. Isham Beard and Elizabeth Curry. Archibald Curry, surety.

Book E

p. 91. Nov. 11, 1835. John T. Dorsey and Mary F. Bass. Thos. Merryman, surety.

p. 179. Feb. 7th, 1837. George Rapale and Frances M. Glass. Isaac Webster, surety.

p. 221. July 10, 1837. James C. Dorsey and Eunice Vining. Samuel Woods, surety.

Book F.

p. 61. April 13, 1841. B. S. Hullum and Mary S. Savoy. Dugald A. Cameron, surety. Married by Egbert I. Sessions, J. P. April 14, 1841.

Book G

p. 81. Sept. 14, 1850. Samuel Swanson and Ruthie Ann Runnels. Married same day by Edward Parker, J. P.

p. 109. April 9, 1851. George Barnes and Louise Nailor. Geo, W. H. Shaifer, surety. Married same day by C. K. Marshall, M. G.

p. 611. Oct. 12, 1851. Frank Nailor to Mary C. Gee.

Book H

p. 135. May 1868. G. Howard Dorsey and Julia Tilman. Geo. Birchett, surety.

p. 445. Nov. 25, 1873. Louis F. Hullum and Louise Dorsey. John Mattingly surety. Married by Robert Price, Minister.

Book H.

p. 497. Mch. 10, 1874. Horace Rhodes and Delia Dixon. Humphrey Moody, surety

p. 595. Feb. 23, 1876. J. Barnes James and Miss Jennie Brook. Dr. R. A. Quin, surety. Married Feb. 24th, by Robert Price, Minister.

p. 651. July 7, 1877. Jefferson Nailor and Minnie Hyland.

p. 644. March 1877. Edw. N. Dorsey and Mary Hullum. L. F. Hullum, surety.

p. 674. Jan. 10, 1878. Louis F. Hullum and Eliza Barnes. Edw. N. Dorsey, surety. Married same date by C. K. Marshall, M. G.

Book I.

p. 41. Dec. 5, 1881. Peyton Harrison and Hattie Barnes. T. Tonnella, surety. Married Dec. 15, 1881 by Rt. Rev. W. F. Adams.

p. 101. May. 3, 1883. Frank Barnes and Virginia C. Ready. W. R. Speers, surety.

p. 233. Sept. 13, 1886. W. H. Land and Ella Armstrong. John Grammer, surety

p. 336. Feb. 1889. Albert L. Dorsey and Mattie G. Wade.

p. 345. June 11, 1889. Henry M. Rhodes and Amelia Battle.

*   *   *   *   *   *

Nos.   Probate Files

4. Nathaniel K. Gibson, Stephen Gibson, admr.

13. Anthony Glass, Andrew Glass, exr.

17. Anthony Glass, Daniel Burnett, gdn.

18. Betsy Glass, Daniel Burnett, gdn.

19. James Glass, Mary Glass, gdn.

28. Malachi Gibson, Martha Gibson, extrx.

29. Clarkey Gibson, Tobias Gibson, gdn.

30. James Gibson, Claudius P. Hicks, gdn..

45. Tobias Gibson, Rachel Booth, admx.

48. Stephen Gibson, Martha Gibson, extrx.

62. N. C. Gibson, Patrick Sharkey, admr.

63. Levi Gibson, Wm. Lewis, gdn.

68. Jordan Gibson, Patrick Sharkey, admr.

86. Henry Bradford, Murphy Bradford, admr.

112. Mary Glass, Jacob Hyland, gdn..

113. James Glass, Jacob Hyland, gdn.

114. Andrew Glass, Mary Glass, admx.

115. Anthony Glass, Anthony Glass, gdn.

128. Clarkey Ann Gibson, James Gibson, gdn.

130. Levi Gibson, Jacob Hyland, gdn.

131. Nathaniel Gibson, Jacob Hyland, gdn.

135. Murdock McLeod, Andrew Glass, admr.

145. Jeremiah Thompson, John Thompson, admr.

183. Henry D. Downs, A. C. Downs, admr.

185. Carolina Downs, Thos. Griffin, gdn.

198. Jordan Gibson, Anthony Durden, admr.

806. Wm. Downs, H. D. Downs, admr.

308. Mary J. Downs, Shem L. Daniel, gdn.

310. Ambrose Downs, Thos. Ferguson, admr.

318. A. D. S. Dillingham, Nancy Dillingham, gdn. of minors.

452. Owen Rhodes, S. T. Rhodes, admr.

468. Edward Swanson, Robt. Garland, exr.

631. Emily Rhodes, Jacob Brump, gdn.

681. Edward L. Downs, Carolina M. Ferguson, gdn.

1157. John Rhodes, Wm. McGarragh, gdn.

1226. Sarah Ann Selser, Jno. M. Selser, nat. gdn.

1426. Esther Selser, Jno. A. Durden, admr.

1446. John M. Selser, Jno A. Durden, admr.

1466. Adelia Selser, Jno. A. Durden, gdn.

1467. Drucilla E. Selser, Jno. A. Durden, gdn.

1986. Mary Gibson, Wm. M. Bullock, exr.

1995. Isaac M. Selser, James M. Selser, admr.

2183. Benj. S. Hullum, Mary H. Hullum, admx.

2189. Joel Hullum, Margaret Hullum, gdn.

2190. Lewis Hullum, Mary Hullum, gdn.

2231. James McLaughlin, Pen Hawkins, admr.

2448. Emma Dorsey, S. McD. Vernon, gdn.

2451. Ella V. Strother, Ann E. Strother, gdn.

2556. Fanny Hullum, Margaret Hullum, gdn.

4511. Strother Matthews, Ella Strother, gdn.

4584. Cyrus Dorsey, W. H. Jefferson, admr.

4862. Chas K. Hullum, S. E. Woods, admr.

5598. James M. Hullum, J. H. Hullum, exr.

6785. Adeline Dorsey, Frederick Day, exr.

7479. Chas. G. Hullum, Gertrude P. Hullum, admx.

8781. Joe Dorsey, Jr., Amos Dorsey, admr.

No. 86. Estate of Henry Bradford, dec'd., Murphy Bradford, admr., Alfred Dillingham, John Fryer and John C. Bellew appraisers. Oct. 28, 1832.

No. 318. Estate of A. D. S. Dillingham, Nancy Dillingham, admx. March Term, 1834.
// Mch. 25, 1834. Letters of guardianship of Mary Eliza and Margaret Dillingham
to Nancy Dillingham. // Feb. 27, 1839. Vicksburg. I, Nancy Dillingham, mother of
Mary E. and Margaret Dillingham, minors, do pray and petition the Probate Court
of Warren County to grant the sale of 600 acres in Washington Co., 200 acres of
which is clear and there is a good gin on the place, also the undivided half of
152 acres, and with this sum to settle the debts of the estate which amount to
$20,000, to protect interest of said minors. Signed: Nancy Dillingham.

No. 468. Estate of Edward Swanson, dec'd., Robert Garland, executor. Bondsmen: Thos. D. Downs, Claiborne Steele, and Robt. J. McGinty, May 28, 1833. // Bill of Peter Grimshaw, March 4, 1833: Dr. Swanson's coffin $40.00; grave pellings(palings) $50. painting same. $5.00. // June 1, 1833, Warrant for appraisement to Robert T. Brown, Benj. Hashberger and Wm. Murfee. // Inventory of personal estate of Edward Swanson, dec'd., 26 negroes, named and valued, $11,492. Signed. Benj. Hasberger, Redding B. Harring, and Green B. Long. // Account of Mrs. Margaret Swanson with R. Garland. Passage of self and servant on "Home" from Vicksburg to Louisville $45.00; hack from Portland for self and servant $.75; for hack various times in Louisville $2.00; Fisher's Tavern for self and servant three and one-half days $6.00; paid to young man for going to Louisville in night $1.25; paid Dr. Elston's bill as per receipt $20.00; for coffin, muslin, etc. $30.50; hearse for taking coffin from Louisville (to Glascow) $8.00. Total $154.25. Amount of cash Mrs. Swanson put into my hand $225.00. Credit balance $70.75. // Aug. 30, 1833. William Richardson versus John M. Chilton, guardian ad litem of the infant heirs of Alfred D. S. Dillingham List of interrogations to be asked Mary E. Logan, wife of Wm. G. Logan, resident of Barren Co., Ky., to prove nuncupative will of Mrs. Margaret E. Swanson, dec'd., relist of Edward Swanson. // Sept. 28, 1833. Wm. Richardson testifies that Mrs. Mary E. Logan can prove that Margaret Swanson, dec'd., bequeathed in her last illness a negro boy named Washington to sd Richardson. // Deposition of Mary E. Logan, wife of Wm. G. Logan, Barren Co., Ky., 12 Nov. 1833. She knew Mrs. Margaret E. Swanson and she died about the 21st of June 1833 at the home of Alexander Smoot, in Jefferson Co., Ky. She and her husband, Wm. G. Logan were present at the time of her death. Just before she died Mrs. Swanson said that it was her will and desire that Dr. Richardson should have her negro boy named Washington and she requested Wm. G. Logan and his wife, Mary, to take notice that such was her will, as Dr. Richardson was a favorite with her. (signed) Mary E. Logan. // Sept. Term. 1834. Further inventory of the estate of Edward Swanson, dec'd. Amount of last inventory and appraisement $10,492. Net proceeds of 78 bales of cotton produced in 1833, $3,038. A long list of accounts due. Total $15,499. Desperate $249,50. // Receipt. Vicksburg, 25 May , 1836. Rec'd. of Robt. Garland, executor of the will of Edward Swanson, dec'd., $360 for nine months service as overseer on the plantation of the late said Edward Swanson on Deer Creek, Apr. 1, 1835 to Jan. 1, 1836. Signed: Daniel Hightower. // Final settlement and allowance, 26 Sept. 1836. Mostly papers on accounting with Blackwell and Swanson who also had a firm at Manchester, nothing coming to the estate from the firm.

No. 2563. Petition of Mary H. Hullum that Benj. S. Hullum died August 1863, leaving the issue of the petitioner, namely: Kate Mattingly, 23, John Hullum, 21, Lewis, 19, Benj. 16, Charley 15, Henry 12, Mary 10, Duke and Walton, twins, 7 and Green 4. July 1866. Her bond as guardian of the minors, for $1000, with L. D. Hullum as surety. (Note: She was Mary H. Savoy, daughter of Samuel Savoy.)

No. 145. Estate of Jeremiah Thomson, John Thomson, admr., May 1819. Advertisements July 12, 1819. Bill for prescriptions, Jan. 20, 1819, again Mch. 8, 11, 13 and 24 1819, for ether and lard, purgative pills and digitalas, from J. A. Maxwell, Claiborne Co. // Mch. 31, 1819. Estate of Jeremiah Thomson to John Thomson, admr. Paid judgment in Warren Co., $153.94 and taxes $5.86. // In 1818, cloth, buttons, silk and bobinet on a bill indicates that his wife, Nancy, was living then. (She was in the 1816 state census of Warren County.)

No. 31. March Term, 1834. Bond of Nancy Dillingham, signed by Claiborne Steele and Wm. L. Sharkey, for $10,000 for admr. of estate of Edward Swanson. Letters of guardianship of Mary Eliza and Margaret Dillingham to Nancy Dillingham, Mch. 25, 1834. Feb. 27, 1839, Vicksburg. I, Nancy Dillingham, mother of Mary E. and Margaret Dillingham, minors, petition the Probate Court of Warren to grant the sale of 640 acres in Washington Co., 200 acres of which is cleared and there is a good gin on the place; also the undivided half of 152 acres, with the sum to settle debts of the estate, which amount to $20,000 to protect interest of sd minors. Signed Nancy Dillingham.

p. 11. Whereas Jeremiah Thomson, late of this county, dec'd., having whilst he lived and at the time of his death diverse goods, rights and credits within the county and state and leaving no last will and testament, John Thomson apptd. administrator. Bond for $10,000, with Andrew Glass and Henry D. Downs, Sr., sureties.

p. 28. John Rail, guardian of Willis and James Sharp, minor heirs of Armistead Sharp, Oct. 25, 1819. with Russell Smith and Murphy Bradford sureties.

p. 53. Bond of Russell Smith as gdn. of Elmer Smith, Benj. F. Smith and Meranda Smith, children of Lucius Smith, dec'd., Henry D. Downs and Andrew Glass sureties.

p. 77. Wm. Bennett, admr. of estate of Solomon Hamon, Sept. 27, 1824.

p. 129. Pharoah Knowland, admr. of Dan'l. C. Jordan, dec'd., with Anthony Durden and James Gibson, sureties. Oct. 8, 1821.

p. 141. Levi Gibson, infant heir of Stephen, dec'd., Oct. 8, 1821. // p. 144. Nath'l. Cloud Gibson, Evaline Gibson and John B. Gibson, infant heirs of Stephen Gibson, dec'd.

p. 162. Murphy Bradford, admr. of Henry Bradford, with Russell Smith and Green Edwards on bond for $1600.

p. 172. Will of Murdock McLeod, my children by first wife; my present and loving wife and son, Malcom. Mch. 31, 1821. Andrew Glass appointed exr. 25 Feb. 1822. Alexander and Sarah McLead, heirs under age of 21.

1823 - 1827

p. 1. Will of William Booker. Beloved wife, Susan, my two infant children, James Booker and Sally Booker. Exrs. wife Susan and Allen Sharkey. Nov. 1822. Prob. April 1823.

p. 5. Foster Cook, admr. of Andrew Glass, dec'd., with Jacob Hyland and Russell Smith, sureties. Sept. 23, 1823.

p. 21. Anthony Glass, admr. de bonis non, of Anthony Glass, Sr., dec'd. Inventory, etc. Sept. 23, 1823.

Wills

Book A

p. 25. Will of Edward Swanson, March 3, 1833, weak in body, my whole estate, negroes stock, land, tenements, accts., etc.. to my beloved wife, Margaret E. Swanson. My trusty friends, Josiah C. Smith and Robert Garland, executors. Signed. Witnesses: David Gibson, A. D. S. Dillingham. (Note: Edward Swanson was buried the 4th March, 1833 and Josiah C. Smith died April 3, 1833, "from cholera" as the others probably did. Margaret Swanson died June 21, of that year in Kentucky, where she went after her husband's death. (File 468). Her brother, A. D. S. Dillingham, having died earlier in June that same year.)

p. 293. Jefferson Nailor's Will. In feeble health, to son, Jefferson, land on Silver Creek in Yazoo County, (in event of his death without children, this land to go to Louise Barnes' children,) also following slaves (65, all named), 22 slaves to Louise Barnes or her children; names slaves that Louise Barnes has already and is to keep, quite a number; grandson, John A. Barnes, grand-daughter, Eliza Barnes, and to my dear little Hattie Barnes. Wife, Eliza to keep this homestead during her life, to be divided between our two children; wife to have entire control of property until son attains age of 21, then he is to pay her $5000 a year and she she is to have the house servants (names five). If son leaves no children, from property I leave him to pay my brother, D. B. Nailor, $20, 000 in two annual payments. George Barnes and D. B. Nailor, exrs. without security. 21 Jany. 1861. I join my husband in the above. Eliza Nailor. Wit: Randal Gibson, Jas. P. Porter, H. H. Hubbard Gideon Gibson.

Book B.

p. 75. Will of Wm. T. Balfour, M. D., of Vicksburg, March 22, 1822. (?. He is in the 1830 Census.) Wife, Emma, extrx. and to have all I have. She is the only one interested; no bond required.

p. 133. Samuel Savoy's will, 2 Oct. 1842, wife Mary, children, Mary H., Lewis and Elmina. Son, Lewis exr. Wm. Fortner gdn. of dau. Elmina. Wit:Maria Jane Owen, Benj. F. Owen, W. L. Sharkey. // Probated Nov. Term, 1842.

p. 211. Will of Peyton Harrison, of Vicksburg, 24 May, 1888, creates a trust for the use of my children, with Thos. M. Smedes, of Vicksburg, Robert Smith and Virginia Smith, of Edmonds, Hinds Co., Miss. They to have entire control over the persons and property of my children. At my death they are to receive American Legion of Honor $5000 and from Knights of Pythias $2,000 and I charge them to educate them preparatory to college and then to put them at a trade as seems best suited and put each in a school where they can learn more about their calling, etc. Wit:W. F. Denson, F. W. Prested. Probated Nov. 9, 1888.

p. 474. Will of Jane L. Brooke, of Vicksburg. My children, Lucy B. Mathews, Horace M. Brooke, Hugh H. Brooke, Jennie B. James and Mary Brooke, all my estate. Horace M. and Hugh H. exrs, no bond. Dec. 6, 1891. Wit:W. G. Paxton, H. C. Kuykendall and S. D. Robbins.

p. ---. Will of Emma H. Balfour, Jan. 29, 1883. Daughter Louise, wife of George M. Klein: granddaughter Alice B. Crutcher.

p. 514. Will of Louise N. Barnes, Dec. 13, 1905. 1/3 of my real estate to dau. Eliza B. Hullum; 1/3 to my son, Dr. John A. Barnes; 1/3 to my dau., Eliza E. Hullum in trust to be managed and controlled by her for the use of my daughter Harriet B. Harrison, and at her death divided equally between her two children, Louise and Peyton Harrison. The same division and conditions regarding my personal estate, except small bequests hereinafter made, the share of my dau. Harriet to be held in trust by my daughter, Eliza B. Hullum, also the portrait of my grandmother, Mary Burnet Anderson and my brother Jefferson Nailor; to my son, John A. Barnes my portrait, his father's, my father's portrait and my sister's portrait taken by Powers. I have given him his part of the silver. To dau. Harriet B. Harrison, my sister's portrait taken by Wigan, and all the balance of the silver, except the large ladle to my granddaughter, Louise Harrison and the small ladle to Elise Barnes. My dau. Eliza B. Hullum, extrx without bond. (Wintergreen Cemetery, Port Gibson, Miss. "Louise Nailer, b. March 9, 1830; Oct. 25, 1906. George S. Barnes, b. Sept. 14, 1829; d. July 21, 1875.")

Book C.

p. 174. Will of Jennie Brooke James, in right mind and perfect health, and good will towards my own and mother's family and a strong sentiment that the home shall be kept as my mother wishes it, leave my interest in my home to my brothers, Horace Miller Brooke and Hugh Holmes Brooke, and my sisters, Lucy Brooke Mathews and Mary Brooke, and an interest to my dear son, Dan A. James for life only, to go back to my sisters and brothers. Should any of the others be dead their interest shall go to Lolla Eggleston, dau. of my sister, Sarah Page Jones. This will made with the intention of keeping the home in the Brooke family. Signed:Jennie Brooke James. Aug. 23, 1905. Wit:C. C. Hurlbutt, Geo. W. Eggleston. Codocil, May 28, 1915. Cash in bank or loaned to be paid to family for use of our home at rate of $20 per month. // Filed Aug. 1916.

Book 1.
p.58. Robt. L.Walton, of Vicksburg, to Moses Calvitt, a slave. Mch.13,1826

p.93. Columbus, Miss.,Jany.25,1827. To all whom it may concern: Know ye
that imposing confidence in the ability of Thos. M.Newell, I do hereby
authorize him, the said newell, to practice medecine in this state, in all its
various branches until next meeting of the Eastern Board of Medical Censors.
(signed) J.H.Haun. Received abd recorded Mch.12,1827.

p.144. Jan.1,1828. For $10,000 deed from Sam'l.L.Woolridge to Charles Lynch,
Thos.S.Sterling, D.W.Haley, Harry Long, Robert Steen, Richard Hurst, Wiley P.
Davis and Fountain Winston, being the sum in which, on the settlement of my
account as Treasurer of Mississippi, I was found in arrears and which sum the
above-named individuals, my securities, became liable to pay and have paid,
transfers, etc. land in the district of Choctaw and a lot in Vicksburg.

p.444. Deed. Jacob G.Winger and Eliza,his wife, stand indebted to Richard
Cordell by note for $449.16, payable Mch.22,1831 and said Cornell, for said
note and $100, deeds the mortgaged land to J.C.McBee,240 acres 'n Hinds Co.

p.505. May 18,1831. Joseph C.Dixon to Robt.McCay,both of Hinds Co., for
$1600, 420 acres which had belonged to Gideon Fitz.

p.576. Dissolution of partnership of Lewis B.Fort and George B.Crutcher,
made March 9,1891. July 4,1831. Wit: H.G.Runnels.

p.659. 8 Feb.1932. A.H.Bankston to Henry Smith, lot in Raymond, signed by
A.H.Bankston and Lucy Bankston. Wit: J.P.Gilbert.

p.673. Vardry McBee, of Lounds County, for $300 to Walter W.New,of Hinds,
two tracts in Hinds. Signed. Wit: T.M.Tucker. Mch.25,1832. Dower rights
relinquished by Alice C.McBee, wife of Vardry. Wit: T.M.Tucker.

p.717. 24 May 1832. Henry Smith, of Hinds Co., to Wm.Lucas, of Franklin Co.,
Ala.,above lot. Signed. Wit: Jas Dawson, M.Coffee, W.W.Lucas.
Book 2.
p.443. Thomas B.J.Hadley, of Hinds Co., Miss., for $39,500 transfers to Harriet
Wooster, of Louisiana, personal property: 35 negroes, named(one Real, the
coachman), all mules, cattle,hogs, and furniture,implements and farming
utensils attached to farm in Hinds County, heretofore occupied and cultivated
by me about two miles from the city of Jackson, reserving only to myself from
the same the marked plate, the tea set of china, yje Piano forte,center table,
beds and bedding, carpenter tools, crosscut saw, grandstone, two horses, saddle
and sulkey horses, wearing apparel and other things as understood between the
parties. Feb.17,1839. T.B.J.Hadley.

p.459. Gift Deed. Thomas Strother, of Hinds Co., for natural love and affection
which I bear to my children, Benj.C.Strother and Prudence G.Strother, $5.00
and slaves. Feb.15,1839.

p.513. 30 Dec.1937. Thos. B.J.Hadley and wife, Piety L.Hadley, to Joel W.
Hardwick, for $1500, one-half of Lot No.3, North, one acre, in City of Jackson.
Signed by both.

p.699. Sedley M.Lynch and Wm.H.Lynch, for $10 and further consideration, five
promisory notes of $4000 each, payable each year from date; for one-third of an
undivided part of the tract of land in Hinds Co.,situated near Jackson, 960 acres,
sold and conveyed by Charles Lynch to Sedley M.Lynch, jointly with William H.
Lynch and Margaret S.Land, by deed, bearing date Mch.2,1840 also to Wm.B.Lynch

(cont.)

Book 2.

p.699.(cont.) an undiveded one-third interest in household furniture and utensils together with all the mules, horses, stock, cattle, etc. and carriages of every description which were conveyed by deed of Chas. Lynch, also one undivided one-third interest in the slaves(Same as those mentioned in following instrument) which are the slaves bequeathed to the mother of, and at her death, to said Sedley M. Lynch, Wm. H. Lynch and Margaret S. Land, formerly Margaret S. Lynch, by their grandfather, William Bracey, dec'd., which slaves are in the possession of Charles Lynch, on hire for the term of five years. (Signed) Sedley M. Lynch. Delivered in the presence of State of Miss. High Court of Errors and Appeals. (S. C. Hist. and Gen. Mag., Vol. 27, p. 225, Married at the High Hills of Santee, June 14, 1804, by Rev. John M. Roberts, Mr. Chas A. Lynch, of Ky., and Miss Ephatha M. Bracey, youngest daughter of William Bracey, Esq.

p.700. Chas. Lynch, of Hinds County, Miss., to Joseph Cooper, William C. Richards and Anselm Lynch, of same, for $10,00uand other considerations hereinafter named, sell and convey in trust for purposes hereinafter mentioned, the following tracts of lands in Holmes County on Honey Island, 1342 acres on which tracts of land Chas. Lynch has established a cotton plantation, also one other tract of land also in Holmes Co., 845 acres, here also Chas. Lynch has cotton plantation, growing crops of cotton, corn, etc., all horses, mules, oxen, cattle, hogs, wagons, carts, ploughs and slaves(too numerous to list). This deed is made for purposes: whereas Chas, Lynch is indebted to the Union Bank of Miss. for $38,800, and to Planters for $19,000, and to the Agricultural Bank of Miss. for $68000 and to Sedley M. Lynch, William H. Lynch and Margaret S, Land, until the whole amount has been paid. It has been agreed that the property is to remain in control of Chas. Lynch. Mch. 1840.

Book 3.

p.261. Jan. 1, 1834. Robert McCay and Eliza, his wife, both of Hinds Co., for $3200, to Sam'l. C. Faulkner, of same, a lot in Clinton, bounded by lot belonging to Gideon Fitz and on east by Wm. S. Lawson. Signed by both.

p.530, Apr. 1835. H. W. Dunlap and wife, Susanna W. Dunlap, to Wm. F. Smith and Peter G. Goosey, for $1000, 8 quarter sections of land, (listed), and 49 slaved(named). Wit: Fisher A. Hamun, Alexander Dunlap.

Book 4.
p.267. Nov. 8, 1831. Hugh McGowan to Robert McCay, for $2,000, tract of 240 acres.

p.564. Jan. 2, 1836. Deed of Trust. Robert McKay and wife Eliza, to Henry S. Foote, tract of land on which Robert and wife, Eliza, now reside, 561 acres with all personal chattles, designated in contract between the parties and Sam'l. C. Faulkner, of Clinton, $26,000. Signed by both.

Book 6

p.532. Order of Orphans Court authorizing Caroline C. McBee, (admx. of Joshua C. McBee), of Hinds County to sell Sarah Calvet certain real estate advertised in town of Clinton, to which Joshua C. McBee had right and title, and whereon the decedent last resided, 120 acres about one mile north of Clinton, for $3600. Dec. 15, 1832. Thos. H. Williams acknowledges the above.

p.506. Dec. 15, 1832. Caroline C. McBee, of Hinds Co., to Sarah Calvit, of Jefferson Co., for $10.00 all her (Caroline's) right, title and interest, and dower and right of dower to west one-half of Sec. 17, Township 6, Range1, West 3/10. (signed) Caroline C. McBee. Acknowledged Dec. 29, 1832.

Book 7.

p. 118. 14 Dec. 1836. T. B. J. Hadley and Piety, his wife, of the first part
to Robt. A. Patrick, all of Hinds County, for $1000, 160 acres (described)
in Choctaw District. Signed by both. Ack. by both in court at Jackson,
Dec. 15, 1836.

p. 476. Sarah D. Terry, dec'd., by administrator, to Edward Wells. Feb. 1st,
1837. Edward Wells, give deed of trust on this property to J. W. N. A.
Smith, admr. of Sarah Terry, dec'd. Feb. 6, 1837.

Book 10.

p. 361. 19 Feb. 1838. Deed from Wilson Gilliland, of Hinds Co., Miss., to
Robert Jones of the town of Utica, Hinds Co., for $100, land in Utica,
Hinds Co, being a part of southeast Quarter of Sec. 8, one-half acre,
more or less. Signed: Wilson Gilliland. Ack. 19thFeb. 1838, before
Wm. W. Floyd, J. P. Recorded 7th February, 1839. S. S. Scott, Clk.

Book 15.

p. 211. Jany. 31, 1842. Edmond Smith and his wife, Ann Smith, now of
Madison Co., and lately of Hinds and formerly of Amite, to Tilghman
M. Tucker, of Loundes Co., for $2,000 in hand paid by T. M. T., land
situate lying and being adjoining the City of Jackson, County of Hinds,
being fully known in survey of public lands, by being the SW 1/4 (ex-
cept a square of ten acres in the SE corner thereof, heretofore sole
and conveyed to Wm. P. Grayson, Esq.) of Sec. 34 T6 R1E, 150 acres.
Signed by both. Ack. in Madison County before Wm. Montgomery, Clk.,
Jany. 31, 1842. Filed Feb. 5, 1842. Recorded Feb. 8, 1842, by John L.
Stubblefield, Clk.

Book 18.

p. 277. 5th Oct. 1846. Power of Atty., from Obedience Smith, of the County of
Galveston, State of Texas to Hiram G. Runnels, of the same county and state.
As my lawful attorney to settle and arrange all my business in the State of Miss.
etc. Signed: Obedience Smith. Ack. 5th Oct. 1846 before Robt. D. Johnson, Commissioner in and for the State of Texas, appointed by the Governor of the State.
to take acknowledgments of deeds, etc.

p. 278. Suit of Robert A. Patrick vs Thos. B. J. Hadley et al. Obedience Smith filed
a cross bill. It was decreed that the land in question by sold at public sale, 30
March 1846, 640 acres in Hinds County. Obedience Smith was the highest bidder,
at $1400.

p. 280. Obedience Smith, of Galveston, Texas, by her atty. sells above tract to
Alexander Virden and Nathaniel Moore for $3200, 30 Nov. 1846. ($1000, cash)
(Obedience, widow of Major David Smith, of Hinds Co., Miss. died in Houston,
Texas, March 1st, 1847.)

Book 23.

p. 308. Jany. 1, 1853. Power of Atty from David S. Terry to Benj. F. Terry.

pp. 317-318. Feb. 27, 1854. Heirs of Sarah Terry to Wm. Mitchell, quit claim
deed, for 1/4 NF and 1/4 SE of NE 1/4 (that is E1/2 of NE1/4)

Book 1.

p. 34. Sept. 16, 1853. F. S. Hunt and wife, Nancy, of Hinds Co., to Lucy A. Morgan,
of Jackson, Hinds Co., for $600, an undivided moiety of the lot on which Austin
Morgan resides, Signed F. S. Hunt, Nancy Hunt.

Book 2.

p. 102. Nov. 5, 1870. Wm. L. Ware and Mary S. Ware, his wife, of Hinds Co., Miss., to Edward Richards, of same, for $4100, tract in Jackson, Hinds Co., 6 acres. Signed by both and ask. Jany. 2, 1871.

p. 184. Dec. 2, 1868. James Lynch, of Hinds Co., to George Washington, Charles Caldwell and Lafayette Coates, of Clinton, Hinds Co., for $10, one-fourth of an acre in the northwest corner of a two-acre tract purchased by sd Lynch of Dr. George Stokes and wife, on northeast by Raymond-Clinton Road, for Methodist Church. (signed) James Lynch.

p. 240. April 13, 1871. William H. Land and Mary J. Land, his wife, to Erwin Lewis, of Hinds Co., for $1300, 127 acres in Hinds Co., Township four. Both signed and acknowledged same Apr. 19, 1871.

p. 346. Dec. 18, 1871. Mary E. McCay and Sam'l. J. McCay, her husband, of Vicksburg, Warren Co., and Wm. B. Mower, of Hinds, of 1st part, and Wm. C. Wells, 2nd part and Sam'l. M. Shelton, 3rd and last part, the last two of Hinds Co. Whereas parties of the 1st part are indebted to party of 3rd part for $325 due on or before March 1st, 1872, as a fee for services to be rendered by him as solicitor for preparing and arguing in Chancery Court for 2nd Dist. of Hinds Co., exceptions to the final settlement of the accounts of the accounts of the exors of the last will and testament of Wm. B. Mower, dec'd., under which will and testament, the said Mary E. McCay and Wm. B. Mower, Jr. are divisees; for $10, sell to 2nd part tract of land in Hinds Co. all of which property belonged to the Wm. B. Mower, dec'd.

p. 467. Jan. 5, 1872. Wm. Caldwell, Wm. Rutland, Sarah A. Rutland and T. M. Caldwell, Jane Caldwell, Robt. A. Travis, R. M. Caldwell, S. E. Caldwell and D. P. Caldwell, heirs at law of J. H. Caldwell, dec'd., to Mrs. Mary P. Walton, of Tennessee, for $100, quit claim in Hinds Co., 160 acres, the same lands having been allowed as dower interest of said Mary Walton in the lands of John H. Caldwell, dec'd., by Probate Court of Hinds County, Miss., Jany. 8, 1869. (signed) Wm. Caldwell, atty. for Wm. Rutland, Sarah A. Rutland, T. M. Caldwell, Jane H. Caldwell, Robt. A. Travis, R. M. Caldwell, S. E. Caldwell and D, P, Caldwell.

p. 510. May 2, 1872. Mary E. and S. J. McCay, her husband, and Wm. B. Mower to John Tougher, of Hinds Co., township 6, 80 acres, for $400. All sign. Ock. May 2, 1872.

p. 511. Mortgage. $200. W. H. Land to G. W. H. Allen and Co., on crop for 1872, 2 horses, oxen and wagon. March 30, 1872. Signed W. H. Land.

                                        Marriage Licenses

Minute Book 1. June 9, 1823-1836.

p. 1. 1st lecense. James Lock to Jane McRara. A. France Sec. 9 June 1823. John W. N. A. Smith, Register.

p. 86. Hosea H. Runnels and Elizabeth Wilson. 31 May, 1830. Wm. D. Wilson, Sec.

p. 211. Wesley Bowles and Sarah Ann Walton. 22 Aug. 1832. Geo. W. Walton, Sec.

p. 169. Jacob B. Morgan and Manerva Fitz. Nov. 7, 1831. F. W. Baird, Sec.

p. 219. Walter Strother and Prudence Yeiser, Sept. 25, 1832. Wm. Bridges, Sec.

p. 501. Jesse Morgan and Eleanor Nichols, 31 Aug. 1836. James Bryant, Sec.

Book 3.

p. 102. James J. Chewning and Miss Minerva Morgan. A. J. Paxton, Sec. Feb. 7, 1850.

p. 74. Wm. A. Ware and Mrs. Sarah M. Land. Jany. 2, 1843. Wm. H. Lynch, Sec.

Will Book 1.
p.   Will of Peterfield Jefferson, Hinds Co., Miss. Appoint my dear and beloved
wife, Elizabeth Howard Jefferson, Extrx. Children to be educated as liberally as
estate and institutions of county will admit. Estate to be equally divided between
wife and children. Portion given to my daughters to be given free from control
of any husband they might have. If either of my children die, to survivor.
Children to be reared according to Protestant Episcopal Church in U.S. Oct. 24,
1850. Wit: George G. Banks, O. L. Nash, R. M. Saunders. Prob. 1852.

p. 334. James D. Ware's Will, of Hinds County, Miss., in feeble health. (1) All my
negroes, stocks, "my Tinnen tract of land", land on Pearl River occupied at present
by my brother, M. Pendelton Ware, to be sold for best interest of the estate. (2)
Little tract on Society Ridge, bought of Dr. J. A. Cotton, I bequeath to my friend,
Abram Owens, of Hinds County, as a home for himself and family. (3) The interest
I claim in the Brunswick Landing Tract of land on the Mississippi River which has
been in litigation in Chancery Court of Miss. at Jackson for some years, I bequeath
to my friend, Burr Garland, if anything should be recovered from said suit. (4)
To Dr. M. Pendleton's two daughters, Susan and Sarah, living in Rockbridge County,
Va., I bequeath a debt due me from their father of $1000, it being a draft Dr.
Pendleton drew on me. This amount I desire him to pay the two girls without
interest in the lifetime of the Doctor, if he should feel able to do so; if not,
to be paid them from his estate after his death. (5) The children of Col. Wm. H.
Garland, of New Orleans, by my late niece, Francis Ann Eubanks, I bequeath the
amount of the debts due me from their father amounting to $2000. (6) To each of
the children of my deceased brother, Dr. Wm. A. Ware, I give the sum of $100 which
I desire be invested by my executors in some suitable memento as a token of my
affectionate regard for them. The large amount of property they will in all prob
ability receive from their mother makes it unneccessary for me to do more for
them. (8)(sic) To my brother, M. Pendleton Ware of Hinds Co., Miss. $5,000 from
the first cash after my debts are paid, to enable him to engage in some commercial
business in Brownsville, Tenn., to which place I so earnestly advise him to remove
and settle for life. (9) To the little son of my deceased brother, A. H. Ware, living
in the county of Madison and for whom I am now guardian, I give $1000. (10) To
my brother, Garland P. Ware, of Louisiana, my gold watch in token of my affectionate regard for him. He does not, I am sure, desire more of me. (11) To my brother,
K. S. Ware, of the State of Wisconsin, $3000 to be paid Jonah Marvin, Esq, as trustee,
to be invested by said Marvin in the purchase of a house for my said brother and his
family. (12) To my affectionate sister, Mrs. Mary Eubanks, of Hinds County, I bequeath
the whole amount of the debt due me from her husband, also $8000. (13) To my
affectionate sister, Mrs. Ann Peebles, of Brownsville, Tenn., $7,000 and the proceeds
of sale of negro girl Jane which I had formerly given and which I lately brought
from Tennessee to sell for her, the said amount to be paid into the hands of my
brother, John D. Ware, of Brownsville, Tenn., as trustee for the use of my sister and
her children, including Sarah Peebles, a dau. of Mr. Peebles by his first marriage,
all children to share alike at death of my sister. (14) To widow and children of
my lamented brother, Mansfield Ware, late of Brownsville, Tenn., $10,000 to be paid
to R. Y. Langley, and John D. Ware, as trustees, and a further sum of $10,000 to
Thomas Ware, son of Mansfield Ware, because he is crippled, for his education.
(15. To my brother, Jno. D. Ware who has a large family, $16,000 in addition to what
I have already given him. (16) Residue of estate to be divided into three equal
parts; one third to Thomas Ware (son of Mansfield); and his sister, Mary Frances
Langley, a third. (cont. following page).

p.334 cont. to the children of my sister, Ann Peebles, including Sarah, the half-sister
as one of them; and a third for Virginia Eubanks, Cornelia Eubanks and Ada Eubanks,
youngest daughters of Mrs. Mary Eubanks and to the orphan child of my friend, Harvey
Stewart, to share alike. John D. Ware and M. N. Eubanks executors. Signed: James D.
Ware. Nov. 18, 1853. Probated Feb. 1854. Wit: Philip Hilsheim, J. W. Shaw, Jno. I. Guion.

p.437. Rockbridge, Allum Springs, Rockbridge Co., Va. July 23, 1856. Memo for will
of Sedley M. Lynch. Exrs: George M. Barnes and Wm. J. Bracey. (1) $2000 to Miss
Ellen Hay annually as long as she remains single. (2)$1000 to be put aside as a
contingent fund to be applied to the relief of my sister should any casualty happen
by which her income will be rendered insufficient to support her in the style and
manner which she has been accustomed to and to educate her children. (3) $1000
each to my cousins: Augustus J. Bracey, Xenephon Bracey, Orlando L. Smith, the
first two of Hinds County and the last of Louisville, Ky. (4) Ample salary to exrs.
to include service also to my sister. (5) At end of five years if Miss Hay has not
married a lump sum of $10,000 to be given her, no more annual payments or
reservations. Any balance to go to Sedley L. Bracey, son of Augustus Bracey. The
whole estate to be divided between nephews, William L. Ware and Sedley L. Ware.
Incase of their deaths, to Cousins A. J. Bracey, Wm. J. Bracey, Xenephon Bracey and
Orlando L. Smith. Signed. Sedley M. Lynch. Wit: George W. Burns. Probated Dec. Court,
1858. Writing identified by Joshua Green, Philip Hilzhein and D. Shelton.

p.450. Will of Mrs. Margaret Ware. Philadelphia, Pa. Will attested by Gustavus
Reichhelm, physician to Mrs. Margaret S. Ware, of Hinds Co., Miss. at the time of
death and for two years previous. 12 July 1859. She died Mch. 1859 in Philadelphia,
where she had resided for two years. // Same from G. W. Mullin, one of the proprietors
of the St. Lawrence Hotel, Phila. had known her for two years. // Same from Wm. S.
Campbell. // Will of Margaret Ware, of Hinds Co., Miss. but lately residing in Philadelphia. Appoints Wm. J. Bracey and George M. Barnes, exrs. Debt paid. Estate in trust
for maintenance, support and education of my sons, Wm. L. Ware and Sedley L. Ware.
Feb. 18, 1859. Probated in Philadelphia. Filed in Hinds Co., Miss. July 9, 1859.
(Margaret Sarah Lynch married 1st, Wm. Clinton Cage; 2nd, Thomas Land, of Holmes Co.
Miss.; 3rd Wm. A. Ware, of Hinds Co. By her first marriage she had a daughter and
a son, The son died in his youth; the daughter was thrown from a horse after she
was grown and killed. By her 2nd marriage, a son was born a few months after his
father's death, and named Thomas Land, but died in infancy and is buried on the
the Charles Lynch lot in Greenwood Cemetery, Jackson, Miss.)

p.347. Will of David C. Land. "Wounds received yesterday. To Beloved wife, Mary
E. F. Land, negro girl named Adeline, 10 years old, household goods and wages due
me as overseer of Mr. B. F. Fortner. Friend, Wesley Crisler, executor. Sept. 15, 1855.

Probate Records

File 269.
Will of Susan K. Mimms. To husband, George W. Mimms. Sr., all property, 766 acres
more or less. Husband, exr. Nov. 1882. Wit: S. A. Stubbs, Wm. R. Kirby, Mary L. Bolls.
Ack. in court by Mary L. Bolls, 14 Jan. 1884, and by Sarah A. Stubbs, n.d. Ack. by
Dr. W. R. Kirby, 25 Jany. 1884. Dec'd. late of Utica. Feb. 4, 1884. Wm. R. Kirby. Will Bk. 2.

File #61. Dr. Thos. F. McKay's estate. Cowles Meade, guardian of his orphan. Feb.
Court, 1833. Mary E. McKay chooses Gen'l. Cowles Meade as guardian, Apr. 20, 1831.
Cowles Meade guardian of Mary Eliza and Laminda Hinds McKay, orphans of Thos.
F. McKay, Apr. 29, 1831. Tract in Jefferson Co., Miss., 700 acres, b. on south by Chas.
West; by Samuel Scott on west, Wm. Harper on north, and James Stewart on east.
Petition to be allowed to sell. One of the wards is married to Mr. Thos. Woolridge.
Bond $10,000. Statement names other heirs: Mrs. Izella McKay, John McKay. Mary
(cont.)

File #61.(con't.)
Est. of Dr. Thos.F. McKay, cont. Statement 1834. Cash to Mary McKay $17.00;
to Mrs Izelle McKay, March, $240.00, same March 1834, $240.00. Cash to Dr.
Morgan $61.00. Final account. Receipt of Genl. Cowles Meade, guardian of Mary
E. Kavanaugh, late Mary E. McKay, as heir of the late Thos. C. McKay, who inter-
married w th Nelson Kavanaugh, all real, personal, and mixed property which
came into hands of guardian from John McKay, exer. Signed N. Kavanaugh. Clinton,
July 11, 1838. Same as the above for Laminda H. Woolridge, who intermarried with
Thomas T. Woolwidge. Signed by T. Woolridge, Clinton, July 11, 1838.
Cowles Meade charges himself for hiring ten negroes, named, of the estate of Dr.
Thos. F. McKay, hired to Nod Rushing. Alex. McKay, Eli Gardner, Thos. Head and Co.,
Izella McKay, James Hamilton, Jno. Gilliland and Jas Wood, of Jefferson.

File 67. J. C. McBee Estate.
Bond of Carolina C. McBee, as admx of estate of Joshua C. McBee, dec'd., to sell
land, signed by Thos. H. Williams and Joseph A. McRaven. Oct. 22, 1832. Petitioner
ordered to sell tract of land in Hinds Co., on which Joshua C. McBee last resided,
320 acres. Bond void after land is sold as ordered by court. Signed: Caroline C.
McBee.
Caroline C. McBee, admx. of est. of J. C. McBee, dec'd., made application to Orphans
Court for order to sell one-third part of an eight of land in T19, Range 18, adj.
town of Columbus in Loundes Co., also 3/4 section of land on Honey Island, pur-
chased from Doctor Lloyd by said Joshua C. McBee in his lifetime, now belong-
ing to his estate. Approved of the court. Bond for $5000 signed by Carolina C.
McBee, Thos. H. Williams and Jacob B. Morgan.
Appraisers of estate of Joshua C. McBee, Sept. 29, 1831; Landy Lindsey, Raymond
Robinson, Thomas Bratton. Bond of Caroline C. McBee, as admx, of estate of
Joshua C. McBee, $15,00.0. signed by Caroline C. McBee, Thos. Land, W. C. Demos.
Order to sell land a citation to the heirs. Commissioners to divide the estate;
Thos. H. Williams, Benj. Bugg, Richard Cordell, Benj. Whitfield.
Account of chattels of estate of J. C. McBee. (Most of the articles were bought by
Thomas Land, father of Catherine McBee) dated Nov. 1831 signed by Thos H.
Williams, Claiborne Kyle. Inventory of estate, dated Feb. 24, 1831, of all goods
and chattels. Nine slaves. Value $5, 370.31.
Caroline C. McBee, admx of estate of Joshua C. McBee, dec'd., reports having
sold, according to law, the undivided interest of sd McBee to one-third part of
a tract of 79 acres in Loundes County, adjoining the town of Columbus. Same
was sold to Andrew Weir, Dan'l. W. Wright and W. L. Moore on a credit of 12
months from Aug. 27, for $500. The other tract on Honey Island was not sold on
account of sd McBee not having a perfect title thereto. Signed: Caroline C.
McBee, admx. Oct. 22, 1832. S. W. Dickson, Atty. for admx.
Caroline C. McBee, admx of estate of J. C. McBee reports tract whereon dec'd.
last resided in Hinds Co., was sold Dec. 15, 1832 for $3600 to Sarah Calvit, on
a credit of 12 months. (Of the above bondsmen, Thos. H. William's wife was a
sister of the dec'd., Joshua C. McBee, whose widow Caroline C. McBee was the
daughter of Thomas Land and his wife, Elizabeth Morgan, who was related to
Jacob B. Morgan.)

File #1224.

Estate of Celia Strother. A.L. Warren, administrator.
Citation to A.L. Warren to show cause why slaves of Celia Strother, decd.,
which she died in possession of, are not appraised, etc. Also why penalty of
bond should not be raised sufficiently to secure rights of parties interested.
Oct. 11, 1852.
Whereas Walter Strother, late of Claiborne Co., Miss., did convey to the female
heirs of Celia Strother certain property intended by the heirs concerned therein
to have been held by said Celia Strother during her natural life, free from division
or incumbrance except so far as said Celia Strother might choose. And, whereas the
said conveyance appears to have no provision for such life estate contained therein,
entirely contrary to the original tenure and intention, let it be known that we, John
Duncan, who married Elizabeth Strother, one of the heirs, Reuben Jones and Ann Jones
and Thessa Bethea who married Emily Strother and Celia Ann Lowry, once Celia Ann
Strother, all of Claiborne County, Miss. and in consideration of the affection we
bear to the mother of our wives and the affection of daughters for their mother, have
given, granted, etc. to said Celia Strother, a full estate for the life of her, the
said Celia Strother, in and to the following slaves: Polly and her two children,
Christiana and George; Emeline and her three children, Jerry, Sarah and Polly; then
at her death to revert to them. (signed) John H. Duncan, R.B. Jones, T. Bethea.
Sept. 27, 1845. Wit: J.C. Barfield.

Deed. Claiborne Co., Miss. Mch. 30, 1830. Walter Strother, of Claiborne County,
Miss., for natural love and affection for my five sisters to wit: Eliz. Strother,
Ann Strother, Emily Strother, and Celia Ann Strother, and also for the sum of
ten dollars, give, grant, etc., two negro girls, slaves, Polly, about 8 years old,
and Emeline, about 7 years old, with increase. Signed Walter Strother.

Petition of A.L. Warren, Hinds County, Miss. Sept. 6, 1852. Celia Strother, late of
this county departed this life 2nd Sept. inst., leaving no will. She died seised
and possessed of a small real and personal estate, of an undivided interest in a
tract of land near Brownsville in said county; one horse, some cattle, hogs, household and kitchen furniture, plantation tools and growing crop of cotton, corn, etc.,
not exceeding $500. A.L. Warren, the petitioner married the granddaughter of
the said Celia Strother. Besides your petitioner, the said decedent left seven
other heirs, to wit: Walter F. Strother, Thomson Strother, Elizabeth Duncan, Emelie
Bethea, Ann Jones, Benj. D. Strother, Adeline Caskey and Celia A. Smith, most of
whom are not residents of this county, but decedent was a widow at the time of
her death. Asks to be appointed administrator with securities. A.M. McKay and
A,P, Bush.

Probate Court, Hinds Co., Miss. Nov. Term, 1852. Answer of A.L. Warren, admr. of
estate of Celia Strother, to petition of Thomson Strother, filed Oct. 8, 1852, pray-
ing that certain slaves be inventoried as personality of Celia Strother. Admr.
denies that he has failed to do this. As to eleven slaves: March 20, 1830, Walter
Strother gave to his sisters, Eliz., Ann, Emily, Adeline and Celia Ann Strother, two
female slaves, Polly and Emeline and that the said petitioner was not mentioned in
such deed of gift and has no interest in the slaves and the eleven slaves alluded to
were Polly and Emeline and their increase. The Admr. admits that Celia Strother
died in possession of said slaves and had done so for many years under written per-
mission of John Duncan, husband of Elizabeth Strother; Reuben Jones, husband of Ann
Strother and Tressa Bethea, husband of Emily Strother, to whom, with others, the said
were given by Walter Strother. Respondent also states that the said intestate was
during her lifetime guardian for Susan Marie Caskey, dau. of said Adeline Strother,
and is now the wife of this respondent and entitled to her deceased mother's share
of said slaves.

Book A

p. 37. Know all men by these presents that whereas the 2nd article filed as
supplement to the treaty of the United States Government and the Choctaw people
there is granted to me, Jamesachikako, the widdow of Pushmataha, late Chief of
the Choctaw Nation, dec'd., and for my children, four quarter sections of land in
trust and my children, to be located under and by the direction of the President
of the United States, and whereas Martha Moore, Betsy Moore and Haschalahurtibbi,
by his guardian, Rene Logan, who are the only surviving heirs at law of said
Pushmataha, did agree with me in the desire that the said land should be sold
and the proceeds thereof appointed with the purchase of negroes and other property
for our joint benefit, relief and maintenance. Now, know ye that I Imaghoka Widdow
of the said Pushmataha, dec'd., for and in consideration of the sum of two thousand
dollars in hand paid by Charles Land, of the State of Mississippi, the receipt whereof is hereby acknowledged, do hereby grant, bargain and sell unto the said Charles
Land and his heirs and assigns forever, the four quarter sections of land so granted
as aforesaid and all my right, title, interest, trustee or otherwise, of, in, and to the
said land, privileges connected as made by the provision of the supplement to said
treaty, as aforesaid. To have and to hold the said four quarter sections of land and
privileges to the said Charles Land, for the benefit of sd Charles Land and his heirs
against all other person or persons whomsoever, claiming or to claim, or either of
us. I do hereby appoint the said Charles Land my attorney for me and in my name
to act for me and receive from the United States Government or such office as may
be appointed for the purpose, the quarter section of land so granted, and to all
things which it would be lawful and proper for me to do and for the purpose of ob-
taining the possession to said Charles Land. Whereof I have hereunto set my hand
and seal the 3rd day of January one thousand, eight hundred and thirty-four. Signed,
sealed and delivered in the presence of Indulger Pummeyyobaker, (his mark) who
interpreted the same in the Choctaw language.

We the undersigned Martha Moore and Tom Suzara, the guardian of Hachalahurtibbi,
the only surviving son of the above Jamesachikako, widow of Pushmataha, dec'd.,
and the only heir at law of Pushmataha, deceased, do jointly and severally consent
to the foregoing conveyance to Charles Land of the four quarter sections of land
granted to Lunnabaka for her and her children, for the consideration of two thousand
dollars, as aforesaid, etc., as above. 13 January, one thousand eight hundred and thirty-
four. Wit: Rena Ingram, Silas D. Fisher. Martha (x) Moore, Betsie(x)Moore, Hachalahurtibbi, by Rena Ingram, his guardian.

Town of Midway, Choctaw. Personally appeared before me before-named Lunnagaka,
widow of the late Pushmataha, deceased, and Martha Moore and Betsie Moore and
Rena Ingram for Hachakahurtibbi, who severally acknowledged that they signed,
sealed and delivered the foregoing four quarter sections of land, etc. 13 day of
January, 1834. (signed) John F. Vere, Lieut. Co. 3 Inf., Com. of Post. (The Choctaws
seemed to have had two names for both Pushmataha and his widow.)

A notaion on the face of the above record, stating that the purchase of the four
quarter sections of land from the widow and children of Pushmataha, granted him
by a provision in the late Choctaw treaty, was to have been by Charles Land and
Abraham A. Halsey jointly. As far as the Land estate is concerned, it said the
widow and children, with the consent of Halsey, have released their interest
therein to said Halsey. (signed) W. H. Johnson, admr. of the estate of Charles Land.
(W. H. Johnson's wife was Charles Land's sister.)

Book A

p. 42-3. Aug. 24, 1833. Ephraim Loyd, of the Choctaw Nation and Susan, his wife,
to Carolina C. McBee, admx. of estate of Joshua C. McBee, for $3,000, 480 acres
on Honey Island. Signed Ephraim Loid, Susan P. Loid. Wit: A. A. Halsey, Thomas
Myers.

p. 44. Yazoo Co., Miss. Feb. 17. 1834. W. Loyd and S. P. Loyd to J. C. McBee, for
$3,000, to be paid as follows: $1000 in negro property on or before July, two
promisory notes of $1000 each of J. C. McBee, to be paid 12 months, thereafter,
480 acres granted Loyd and wife by General government in a treaty held at
Dancing Rabbit Treaty Creek and signed 27 Sept. 1830. Said reservation of 480
acres to include part of improvement and the dwelling house where the said E. Loyd
and S. P. Loyd resided at the time of the treaty, on the waters of Little River on
Honey Island. We, the said E. and S, P. Loyd bond ourselves to procure a legal
title to same reservation from the U.'S. Government, and convey same to J. C. McBee.
Signed by both, June 11, 1831. Signed C. C. McBee. Wit: Thos. Land, Charles Land.
(Thomas and Charles Land were brothers of Caroline C. McBee.)

p. 45. John Wallace and Polly, his wife, to John R. Wilson, all of Holmes Co., Miss.,
for $2500, tract in Holmes Co. Both signed with marks. Wit: Thomas Lemon, James
Hansed. John B. Maurv, J. P.

p. 45. Dec. 18, 1834. Robert John Walker and Thomas Barnard, of City of Natchez,
Adams Co., having purchased at the sales of public lands at Columbus, a certain
tract in Holmes Co., and having authorized the undersigned to sell same to Mr.
Richard Cunliffe late of the State of Virginia, at a rate of $4 per acre, payable
in equal installments, viz. one-third cash, 2-thirds in one and two years with int.,
the sd Richard Cunliffe having consented to foregoing condition. Signed George
Dougherty. Dec. 5, 1832.

p. 81. Aug. 16, 1834. Indenture between Joseph McAfee, of Covington Co., and the
trustees of Jefferson College, Washington, Miss. Joseph McAfee by Morgan McAfee.
Wit: D. W. Canby, Doris Montgomery.

p. 180. Aug. 13. 1834. I, Joseph McAfee, of Covington Co., Miss., have purchased
from the Trustees of Jefferson College in town of Washington 1280 acres on location,
whereof Joseph McAfee, the purchaser of Jefferson College aforesaid, is aithorized
to make entry upon any of lands of the United States in Mississippi, upon execution
of a deed of transfer from said trustees or their agents. The said Joseph McAfee is
bound by the terms of his purchase to execute a good and sufficient mortgage to
the trustees of Jefferson College. Noe, know ye that I, the said Joseph McAfee
have made as my lawful atty. Morgan McAfee to ask, demand and receive a deed
of transfer of the land purchased from Jefferson College, to be entered according
to Act. of Congress, Apr. 20, 1832 and to mortgage same to Jefferson College to
secure payment price.

p. 232. July 5, 1834. Agreemwnt between Wm. H. Johnson, Caroline McBee and
Charles Land.

p. 528. July 26, 1834. Aug. 1835. Robt. S. Herbert and Martha, his wife, to Joseph
M. Taylor, land in Holmes Co., for $5000. Signed: Kobt. E. Herbert. Martha A.
Herbert.

Book B

p. 28. Recorded July 30, 1837. Indenture, 24 Oct. 1837. Joseph C. Pickens, Edmund Russell, James C. Bole and Rutha A. Bole, his wife, and Hiram G. Runnels
and Obedience A. Runnels, wife of Hiram G. Runnels, to Israel Pickens, for $510
paid by the 2nd part, (Israel W. Pickens), others convey a parcel of land on Big
Black River, 80 acres. Signed by all. Ack. by Hiram G. Runnels and O. A. Runnels
before R. A. Patrick, clerk of High Court of Errors and Appeals.

p. 139 Dec. 1837. Walter Cates, of Holmes Co., Miss., and McEwing King & Co.,
of the State of Miss., for $6240 paid to said Cates by above McEwing King & Co.,
for several tracts of land and slaves for 999 years in yearly installment of $624
at town of Holly Springs, Marshall Co., to above Cates.

Book D

p. 308. Aug. 22, 1839. I, John M. Clement, of Lexington, Holmes Co., for $100, to
James I. McNight of sd Lexington, release and quit claim to lot and building in
Lexington, all interest and claim which I have by virtue of a deed from Israel
Pickens, Sheriff of County, dated Aug. 8, 1839.

p. 309. May 28, 1839 - July 1st, 1839. Thomas Land, of Holmes Co., in consideration
of love and affection I have for my sister, Caroline C. Johnson, gives to sd Caroline
C. Johnson, my beloved sister, land in Holmes Co. Signed Thomas Land. Wit: S. M.
Lynch, W. A. Land. Personally appeared Wm. A. Land, who saw other witness,
Sedley M. Lynch sign as witness. July 1st, 1839. (Thomas Land died June 16, 1839)

Book E

p. 403. Aug. 18, 1839. Walter Cates and Kitty H. Cates, his wife, of Holmes Co.,
to David C, Thomas, for $400, land in Holmes Co., 80 acres.

Book F

p. 161. Sedley M. Lynch, of Hinds Co., to Chas. Lynch, of same. Whereas Sedley M.
Lynch, about 1831 did purchase jointly with Wm. C. Gage, since dec'd., of Jefferson
Montgomery, a tract with plantation, 320 acres, also of James Briley 160 acres
in Holmes County and Sedley M. Lynch did purchase of U. S. Government, 365 acres
more or less contiguous to above, also purchased of Samuel Long $20 acres lo-
cates on Honey Island, also purchased of Indian, widow of Pushmatsha and her
three children, Martha and Bettie and   land in Holmes Co., and 380 acres
of the Govt. The purchase money for the whole above was paid by Charles Lynch,
For $1.00 paid by sd Chas. Lynch, Sedley M. Lynch conveys to Chas. Lynch the
several tracts and improvements. Signed: Sedley M. Lynch. Jan. 1st, 1840.

p. 317. Oct. 9, 1840. Levi Hurlbert to Wm. H. Doty, and Wm. S. Mitchell, for $150,
land described in deed from Osais Taylor and wife to Levi Hurlbert for 99 years
from July 1835. Signed: Levi Hurlbert.

p. 336. 17 Jan. 1867. Joshua T. McBee and Mary D. McBee, his wife, to Pallas
Johnson, all of Holmes County, for $10,000, all of sec. 10, No. 11, west of
Funnygusha, T15 R1E, except one-half acre in sec 10, containing the family
graveyard of W. W. Walton, 875 acres, all of the plantation formerly owned by
estate of F. C. Meade, dec'd., for $7,000 cash, balance a note of Pallas Johnson
and Joseph E. Johnson, her husband. Signed: J. T. McBee, M. D. McBee. Recorded
Jan. 17, 1867.

p. 421. Jan. 22, 1839. James M. Gwin and Susan V., his wife, and Edmund Pursell
and Margaret, his wife, of Holmes Co., to Morgan McAfee, of Tallahatchie Co.,
Miss., $400 paid by McAfee, convey tract of land which Jacon Tipton conveyed
to Wiley Davis and was sold by Sheriff as property of Wiley David to James Gwin
and W. W. Walton and Walton's relict conveyed to sd Pursell. Recorded March 1841

Book F

p. 521. May 16, 1840. Richard P. Watson and Mary, his wife, to Joseph D. Watson
and Susan, daughter of Richard and Mary, who was intermarried with Wm. Anthony,
for $1500 paid by Joseph D. Watson, house and lot in Marion, Perry Co., and the
other half to Susan Anthony, my daughter.

p. 556. 12 July 1841. Wm. Hampton and Sarah Hampton, his wife, A. Lomax, Leroy
Brewer, Luke Powers, C. Foster, Stephen Johnston, J. J. Carnes and Albert R. Harris,
Trustees, for fifty dollars, all interest, claim etc., that Wm. Hampton and wife,
Sarah, have in lot in town of Emery, known as Academy Lot, 4 acres. Trustees
to finish building to use as a place of worship of the Methodist Episcopal Church.

p. 834. William R. Campbell, or Washington, Co., paid $5945.62 by Rutherford C.
Land, of Holmes Co., for a certain judgment recovered in Circuit Court of Holmes
County, Oct. 19, 1840 against Thomas T. Land for $5151.23. Oct. 26. (Thomas Land
married Mary E. Dillingham, who, with her sister Margaret, inherited the estate of
Edward Swanson through the death of his widow, Margaret Dillingham Swanson. The
plantation inherited in what is now Sharkey County was heavily mortgaged to W. R.
Campbell as were many of his holdings. (See Warren County)

Book G

p. 3. Dec. 11, 1839. Indenture between William Oliver, of 1st part; John M. Clement,
Wm. F. Austin, of 2nd part and Wm. McCutcheon of 3rd, all of Holmes Co. Whereas
the party of 3rd part releases to 1st party all right, title and claim in the following
lot and parcel of land in town of Lexington, Holmes Co.: East one-half of Lot 33, on
which is grocery, facing the square; No. one-half of Lot No. 42, on which is a dwelling,
for which he received a promisory note for $875. Lexington. Dec. 11, 1839. 1st party,
Wm. Oliver, mortgages same to John M. Clement and Wm. F. Austin. Signed by all parties
Wit: J. M. Dyer, J. M. Brown.

p. 22. Oct. 1839. Wm H Johnson, of Holmes Co., to Silas McBee, of Pontotoc Co.
Whereas Wm. H. Johnson is indebted to the said Silas McBee for $2000 by promisory
note, dated Jan. 19, 1839, payable Jan. 1st 1840 or before, the said note being given
for a negro man named Sam, slave for life, aged about 50, now sd Wm. H. Johnson
being desirous of securing to said Silas McBee the said sum of $2000 gives deed of
trust on sd slave, Sam, to Silas McBee, until the amount of purchase and interest is
paid. Signed: Wm. H. Johnson.

p. 113. Deed. Sedley M. Lynch, of Hinds Co., to Wm. H. Lynch, of same, for $10.00
and $20,000 to be paid by sd Sedley M. Lynch, for which Wm. H. Lynch has executed
five promisory notes of $4,000 each, bargains, sells and delivers to sd Wm. H. Lynch
the undivided one-third part of the tract of parcels of land, lying and being in the
State and County aforesaid and situated near the City of Jackson, containing 900
acres sold and conveyed by Charles Lynch to sd Sedley M. Lynch, jointly with Wm.
H. Lynch and Margaret S. Land, by deed dated 2 Mch. 1840, and the said Sedley doth
also sell, etc. to sd William H. Lynch one-third part of household furniture and
utensils, with all the horses, mules, stock of cattle and hogs, farming implements
and carriages of every description, which were sold and conveyed by aforsaid deed
of sd Chas. Lynch, also one-third of undivided part of the following slaves. (52 in
all, named), together with one-third of their increase, which are the slaves and the
increase of the females of the slaves bequeathed to the mother of, and at her death
to the said Sedley M. Lynch, Wm. H. Lynch and Margaret S. Land, formerly Margaret
Sarah Lynch, by their grandfather, William Bracey, deceased, which slaves are in the
possession of Charles Lynch on hire for the term of five years, etc. Signed: Sedley M.
Lynch. Ack. in Jackson, Mch. 10, 1840. Recorded same day.

Book G

p. 279. John C. Jenkins, of Adams Co., for $100, quit claim to land on Honey Island, 2 May 1843, (1840. T. Land to J. C. Jenkins deed of trust on Honey Island. The above was apparently the last payment. // I, Thos. T., exr. of last will and testament of Chas. Land, dec'd., for $650 to John T. Butler, of Natchez, undivided one-half of tract on Honey Island. 26 May 1843.

p. 469. Francis Wyatt and John Wyatt, of Holmes Co., are indebted to Mary E. Land, also of Holmes Co., for $3600, mortgage land, 25 acres, leased to Chas. Eggleston until 1845. Signed: Fr. Wyatt, John M. Wyatt. Wit: W. W. Walton, Thos. T. Land, E. G. Purdom. Filed May 4, 1841. Satisfied Dec. 19, 1844. Rec. May 4, 1841.

p. 516. Whereas in suit recently pending, wherein James R. West and Wm. H. Johnson were plaintiffs and Stephen D. Bell, defendants, by Circuit Court held Oct. 1841, the said James R. West and Wm. H. Johnson recovered judgment for $677.13 with interest from Oct. 27, 1841. Sheriff's sale of land, 155 acres, to John M. Clement, highest bidder for $10. Oct. 18, 1843. John D. Wyatt, Sheriff.

p 567, Nov. 12, 1842. Thos. T. Land, sole acting exr. of last will and testament of Charles Land, dec'd., late of Holmes Co., to Caleb Worley, of Holmes Co., Sam'l. Theobald and Lloyd Warfield, of Kentucky, for $19,200, in hand paid to Wm. H. Johnson, of Holmes Co., late admr., with will annexed of sd Chas. Land, dec'd., in following tract of land, 640 acres, Sec. 25, T16, R1W on Honey Island. Signed: Thomas T. Land, executor of Charles Land.

p. 593. Sheriff's Sale. Feb. 24, 1844. To Mary A. Land and Charles, land of Joseph M. Cordozo, for 61 dollars. (Rutherford's Land's widow and son).

p. 612. Messrs Joseph S. Copes and Robt. Cook convey to Israel Pickens lands with all turnpike and ferry privileges appertaining thereto and one-sixth of ferrage now due the turnpike and ferry known as Bowles Ferry, it being the same conveyed to you on Nov. 6, 1840. Mr. Pickens has this day executed a note to pay J. S. Copes, Esq., $750 due Feb. 1, 1845. You will therefore make conveyance Jany. 27, 1844. Signed H. G. Runnels. Wit: Duncan McEarhern and ack. 11 Mch. 1844 before A. L. Hilman, J. P.

p. 690. Deed. 2 Feb. 1844. Thomas T. Land, exr. of estate of Charles Land, dec'd., to Sam'l. Theobald and Lloyd Warfield, of Kentucky, for $1,000, land on Honey Island, 2 lots on Horse Shoe Lake, part of Sec. 26, T16, 128 acres granted to the heirs of Chas. Land under preemption claim recognized as valid by the Court of United States under act of Congress 1834. Thos. T. Land, exr. of Chas. Land. Wit: W. R. Campbell.

p. 757. Deed. 5 Nov. 1844. William Ridgeway and Harriett E. Ridgeway, his wife, of Holmes Co., Miss., to Thomas Ship for and in consideration of a negro boy named Andrew, aged seven, a slave for life, land in Holmes Co., Lot No. 3, Sec. 14, T15, R3E, 80 acres.

p. 795. 6 Jany. 1843. Thos Land, acting exr of will and testament of Charles Land, dec'd., of Holmes Co., to William A. Land · · · · · ·

p. 811. R. C. Land and Mary A. Land, of Holmes Co., to Jackson Johnson, all rights and title to west one-half of NE quarter of Sec. 9, T15, R10E. . . .

Book I.

p. 94. Deed. Feb. 19, 1871. Silas W. Land, William A. Land, William A. Land, Jr., M. A. Wall and her husband, W. K. Hall, for $125, to James Morris land in Holmes County. Signed: W. A. Land, Sr., S. W. Land, M. A. Wall, W. K. Wall, Wm. A. Land, Jr.

p. 207. R. C. Land and Mary A. Land, his wife, of Holmes Co., to William A. Land, of Holmes Co., for $2000, 640 acres in Holmes Co. (description), Jan. 25, 1847. Signed: R. C. Land, Mary A. Land.

Book I

p. 208. Know all that I, William Ramsey, of Hardeman Co., Tenn., for love and affection, to my daughter, Mahulda Land, wife of Wm. Land, of Holmes Co., Miss. three slaves, John, age 18, Harriet, age 15, and Martha, age 14. Signed: W. Ramsey. Apr. 2, 1847. Wit: J. M. Fletcher, J. H. Hickson. Ack. in Shelby Co., Tennessee.

p. 214. Feb. 13, 1847. State of Texas, County of Bowie, Martha B. Runnels, Hiram J. Runnels, Edmond S. Runnels and Howell W. Runnels appoint Harden Runnels attorney in fact to transact all business in Miss. Acknowledged in Texas. Signed: N. D. Ellis, Commissioner in Texas for the State of Mississippi.

p. 215. The above sell to Hardin R. Runnels all right, title and interest in Lots, No. 10, 11, 12 of Sec. No. 19, T17, R1E, also undivided half-interest in lots 2, 7, 11, 12, 13, 14, 3, 6, 4 & 5, of Sec. 30, T17, R1E, 350 acres, more or less, lying in Holmes Co., consideration $1200. Apr. 2, 1847. Hardin R. Runnels, atty-in-fact.

p. 366. 28 Feb. 1847. Hardin Runnels, of Bowie Co., State of Texas, to Abraham W. McGowan, of Madison Co., Miss., for $1500, 640 acres. Ack. in Madison Co. before John T. Cameron, Clerk of Probate Court. Signed: Hardin R. Runnels.

Book L.

p. 62. Filed Mch. 11, 1850.   Mch. 6, 1850. Ira C. Ash, of 1st part and James M. Wilson, of 2nd part, and Amanda V. Ash and George W. Ash, of 3rd part. Whereas Ira C. Ash is partly indebted to said George W. Ash in the sum of $300 and int. since April last and also to Amanda V. Ash, the wife of Ira C. Ash, in the sum of $250 with interest since 1846 for separate property of Amanda V. Ash, sold and used by Ira C. Ash and whereas the said James M. Wilson is surety of the said Ira C. Ash in a promisory note payable to Mary Ann Shipp for the sum of $400 upon which judgment has been awarded against the sd Ira C. Ash and James M. Wilson in the Circuit Court of Holmes Co. in favor of Mary Ann and Thomas C. Shipp. It is believed by I. C. Ash and James Wilson that they are not justly liable but it is the wish of said Ira C. Ash to endemnify said Wilson as surety. This endenture therefore witnesseth that in consequence of the premises and $10 to him paid by sd Wilson, he grants, bargains and transfers to Wilson and his assigns the tract of land in Holmes Co., known as Ashville, bounded on the north by land of J. N. McLean, south by land of J. B. Walton, east by Wm. Clower, 18 acres, also one small horse and stock of goods on hand, thought to be between $1200 and $1500, also back accounts of Ira C. Ash since Jan. 1st last, amounting to $246 upon condition that Wilson shall collect accounts and have control of goods and shall pay from proceeds the amount of the judgement, if case is reversed, then pay Amanda V. Ash the remainder thereof and after 1st of next June, Geo. W. Ash and Amanda V. Ash shall sell land with apperternances for their debts, subject to Wilson's 1st claim. Signed: I. C. Ash, J. M. Wilson, Amanda V. Ash.

p. 96. Rankin Co., Miss. We, John G. Parker and Eliz., his wife, Wm. M. Jayne and Melissa A. Jayne, his wife, heirs at law of Joseph McAfee, dec'd., do hereby assign right and interest to Morgan McAfee the following tracts in Holmes Co. located by the said Joseph McAfee, of Covington Co., assignee of Jefferson College at Mount Salus land office Aug. 16, 1834. Mch. 6, 1850. Signed: John G. Parker, Elizabeth Parker, Wm. M. Jayne, Jos. M. Jayne, Melissa A. Jayne. Filed Apr. 5, 1850.

p. 105. Hinds Co., Miss., Logan B. Rogan and Minerva Rogan, his wife, transfer our right, title and interest in following tract in Mississippi, lying in Holmes Co., Honey Island, located by Joseph McAfee of Covington Co., assignee of Jefferson College at Mt. Salus Land Office, Aug. 16, 1834. Mch. 1850. Signed by both. Rec. Apr. 5, 1850. (Grantee not given but it is evidently Morgan McAfee. See other deeds.)

Book L.

pp. 107-8. Hinds Co., Miss. Joseph McAfee, of Covington Co., transfers his title etc. to tract of land in Holmes Co. to Morgan McAfee, (same land as in two preceding deeds.) Feb. 21, 1851. Rec. Apr. 5, 1850.

p. 238. Caddo Parish, Louisiana. We, B. F. Eppes and Mary, his wife, J. M. Ford and Frances B. Ford, his wife, E. J. S. Cates and Wm. Y. H. Cates, all of Caddo Parish, for $2590 in promisory notes drawn by Ezra Cates, dated Sept. 11, 1839, to us in hand paid by Walter Cates sell to Walter Cates, of Holmes Co., Miss. our right, title and interest, as heirs of Ezra Cates, dec'd., land in Holmes Co., Miss., and 16 slaves, herein named. Signed by the above heirs of Ezra Cates.

p. 423. Mch. 24, 1850. Joseph Walton and Elizabeth Walton, of Holmes Co., to Mahulda Land, of same, for $100, 10 acres adjoining land sold by Armistead G. Otey to Mahulda Land. Signed by both.

p. 449. Jan. 1, 1810. Madison McAfee and Ann H. McAfee, his wife, to Morgan McAfee, all of Holmes Co., Miss., for $86.30 sell their interest in sixty-nine acres of land.

p. 515. Deed of Trust. Holmes Co., Miss. For $7,000 borrowed by Morgan McAfee, he gives ten negroes to Thos. E. Helm and if the next note, dated May 1, 1851, is not paid, he authorizes Wm. Stansbury to sell said negroes or so many as will satisfy the debt. The said McAfee is also to let said Helm have his entire crop of cotton which he may make this year on Honey Island to be shipped to New Orleans and the proceeds to be placed to credit of Helm and as payment of $7,000. May 7, 1851. Signed Morgan McAfee. Wit: W. L. Thomas.

p. 623. Holmes Co., Miss. Jan. 3, 1852. Morgan McAfee sells to Thos. E. Helm for $400, tract in Holmes Co. Rec. Jan. 3, 1852.

p. 827. John M. Clements, of Holmes Co., for $135, sells to James M. Gwin, tract of land, 45 acres and Margaret C. Clements, in consideration of $1 relinquishes her dower rights. Signed and acknowledged by both.

Book M

p. 25. Mch. 2, 1853. Walker Brooke and Madison McAfee, of Mississippi and L. P. Bayne, of Washington City and Selden Withers & Co., of Washington City. 1st part are indebted to 3rd part for $1500 mortgage on land and negroes. Signed by both and acknowledged before Chas. D. Selding, Commissioner for Mississippi, who was also witness.

p. 67. May 9, 1853. Morgan McAfee to Wm. Trahern who did convey Dec. 8, 1845 to McAfee a tract of land and did warrant title of same. Morgan McAfee releases him from Warrant of title for $500. May 9, 1853.

p. 555. Nov. 13, 1854. Joseph R. McAfee, of Holmes Co., to Madison McAfee, of Hinds County and C. J. McRay, of Mobile, Ala., for $670, 167 acres in Holmes Co. Signed: Jos. R. McAfee.

p. 607. Jan. 10, 1855. Morgan McAfee of Holmes County for $1390, to Wm. M. Jayne, of Rankin, 69 acres in Holmes Co. McAfee ack. in Hinds Co.

p. 739. May 30, 1855. Morgan McAfee, 1st part; Benj. T. Owen, 2nd part; Collins F. Hemingway, Sam'l. Friedlunder and Benj. Gerson (partners in N. O.)3rd part. 1st is indebted to 3rd for $12,000 and mortgages land and negroes.

p. 718. May 1st, 1855. Morgan McAfee to John A. Durden, both of Holmes County. for $400, 80 acres in Holmes Co. Signed. Wit: J. R. McAfee.

Holmes County
Deeds

Book M

p. 118. Jan. 10, 1852. John N. Frizell and Catherine, his wife, to John M. Clement all of Holmes Co., for $200, land in Holmes Co. Both signed. Rec. June 21, 1853.

Book N

p. 414. July 12, 1832, George W. Haskins, of Choctaw tribe of Indians to Charles Land, of Yazoo County, Miss., for $2400, a certain tract that George W. Haskins is entitled to by a treaty of Sept. 15, 1830 of Choctaw people and U. S. Government on east bank of river opposite Honey Island. Wit: C. Morancy, W. E. Cherry. Yazoo County, personally appeared before Sam'l. Atchison, J. P., C. Morancy and acknowledged above. Aug. 11, 1832. (Record in Yazoo Deed Bk. C, p. 300.)

p. 830. Mch. 2, 1857. Commissioner sale of land belonging to estate of Margaret E. Clements, dec'd., according to May term, 1856, sold to Henry K. Jones, highest bidder, for $1585.

Book Q.

p. 450. Release. Know all men by these presents that we, Nancy Rhodes and Margaret Dillingham have allotted and assigned unto Mary E. Land, for her share and full part in the estates of Edward Swanson and Alfred D. S. Dillingham, the following named slaves, to wit: Randal, abt. 50, Hannah, abt 40, and her 8 children: Nash, Bob, Charlotte, Henry Claib, Margaret, Sam, and Ellen, etc. Signed: Nancy Rhodes, Margaret Dillingham, Jany. 2, 1841. Wit: S. G. Galloway. Mary E. Land receipted for same as her share in above estate.

p. 469. Deed of Trust. Mary E. Land, on Francis and John Wyatt, $3500. Mch. 9, 1841. Wit: W. W. Walton, Thos. T. Land, E. G. Purdom.

Marriage Bonds

Book G.

p. 129. D. S. Humphreys to Miss L. S. Hoskins, Apr. 28, 1886. Sec. J. B. Humphreys. Married Apr. 29, 1886 by R. W. Mecklin, V. D. M.

p. 193. D. E. Hoskins and Miss J. W. Highes. Feb 23, 1887. Sec. J. M. Dyer. Married Nov. 20, 1889, by Thos. Y. Ramsey, M. G.

p. 333. T. M. Henry to Carrie M. Pickens. Nov. 17, 1889. Sec. G. W. Stigler. Married Nov. 20, 1889, by R. W. Mecklin, V. D. M.

p. 16. R. K. Jones to Miss C. A. Robinson. Mch. 11, 1884. Sec. J. T. Meade. Married Mch. 12, 1884 by B. Halstead.

p. 113. H. V. Johnson to Miss Ada L. Herbert. Jan. 25, 1886. C. Oltenburg Sec. Married Jany. 26, 1886 by J. F. Evans.

p. 252. Peyton T. Jones to Miss Annie S. Durden, July 19, 1888. M. M. Grant Sec. Married by Thos. Y. Ramsey, M. G.

p. 71. J. Kier to E. M. Hoskins, Apr. 8, 1865. R. H. Baker, Sec.

p. 138. Watt McCain to Miss Sallie R. Cole. May 18, 1886. Sec. G. G. Jones and W. L. Walton. Married by R. W. Mecklin, V. D. M.

p. 192. J. A. Moss to America Walton. Feby 25, 1887. W. L. Walton, Sec. Married by A. P. Pugh.

p. 379 E. F. Noel to Loula L. Hoskins. June 4, 1890. Sec. S. N. Sample. Married by A. P. Pugh.

p. 308. J. C. Pinkerton to Tullia Simmons. Apr. 30, 1889. Sec. W. W. Durden Married by John H. Boyd, pastor Lauderdale Presbyterian Church, Memphis, Tennessee.

Book G.
p. 119. J. W. Sommer to Maggie J. McBee, Feb. 16, 1886. Sec; P. Simmons.
              Married Feb. 18, 1886, by R. W. Mecklin, V. D. M.
p. 156. R. E. Simmons to Virginia McAfee, Dec. 8, 1886. Sec; E. L. Martin.

p. 225. M. L. Stigler and Mi s L. W. Cole, Feby. 6, 1886. Sec: J. M. Dyer.
              Married Feb. 6, by E. S. Cowan, St. Mary's Church
p. 115. W. W. Thurmond to Miss Lida Walton, Jany. 26, 1886. Sec. J. A. Jenkins.
              Married Jany. 27th, by J. T. Ellis, M. G.

p. 185. H. W. Walton to Lula Hamilton, Dec. 18, 1886. Sec. J. M. Dyer.
              Married Dec. 21, by J. T. Evans, M. G.

p. 292. F. A. Wyatt to Mrs. G. C. Cole, Jany 30, 1889. Sec. T. J. Wyatt.

Book H.
         Edwin W. Anthony to Miss Daisy Williams, Aug. 24, 1896; m. Ang. 26th
         John C. Brantley to Ann E. Archer, June 1st, 1896, m. June 3rd.
         Cuddy Thomas Charles to Jennie Robinson Archer, Jan. 16, 1897
              Married Jan. 27, by Stevenson Archer.

         Robert H. Douthat to Miss Maggie P. Simmons, Feb. 28, 1898
              Married same day by Eugene L. Siler, M. G.

         L. T. Dickey to Miss Pallas Kirkland Johnson, July 4, 1878.
              Married July 5, 1898 by Eugene L. Siler, M. G.

         W. I. Pickens to Marie M. Durden, May 30, 1894.
              Married same day by Father W. TenBrink.

         H. W. Brantley to Miss Florence V. Archer, Jan. 23, 1886. Sec. W. B. Jones.
              Married Jan. 29, by B. Halstead, priest.
              *   *   *   *   *   *   *

                                 Wills

Book I.
p. 1. Lewis Leflore's Will. Lewis Leflore, of the Choctaw Nation, State of Miss.
To son Forbes Leflore $700; two nephews, Staphen Crevat and Placide Crevat,
each $300; to my niece, Mary Crevat $300: my children, Greenwood Leflore,
William Leflore, Louisa Hoskins, Felicity, wife of Samuel Long, William McGaley
and Silva Harris, Clarissa Wilson, Isabel Bashersm wife of Vaughan Bashears. Exrs:
Samuel Long and my friend Abraham Halsey. 6th April 1833. Signed: Louis Leflore.
Wit: W. M. Parker, W. W. Cherry

p. 4. Will of Samuel Armstrong, sick and weak. Estate to my wife, Edney, for her
widowhood, then to my only child, Sarah Jane. June 20, 1833. Signed. Wit: Paul
Hughs, Wm. C. Petty, B. A. Oliphant, Jonathan Armstrong.

p. 5. Charles Land's Will. Holmes County, June 15, 1834. My wife and my son
Thomas to have same power that I had myself in lifetime. All the negroes to be
kept together until my son Thomas becomes of age or longer if they think proper.
Rutherford and Martha to be educated out of the estate. My wife is to have the
negroes Ann, Joseph, Daniel and Pres for her lifetime and the land I now live on
containing 160 acres. At her death it is to be equally divided between the three
children. Signed: Charles Land. Wit: Wm. H. Johnson.

p. 9. Will of John Willis. Mch. 22, 1835. My land and improvement being on the
northwest prong of Harling's (Harland's) Creek; my estate to sons, Joseph, Thomas
and Jeremiah and their sister Nancy and two other sisters, Milley and Sarah, all
the rest of my children only $1.00 each, namely: Eliz., Mary, Hannah, John and
James. John (x) Wallis.(sic) Test: Wm. S. Blancoe, J. G. Sims, M. C. Blancoe.

Book 1.

P. 6. Wm. Arick's Will. State of Mississippi. My eldest daughter, Mary Ann Davis,
wife of Aaron B. Davis, if she survive me, if not, to her children should they survive,
certain slaves (named) and land under the direction of executors: to wife, Acenitha,
and my four children, Hannah Arick Hiram Arick, Wm. Arick and Entrude Arick.
Wife, brother-in-law, Hiram G. Runnels and my friend, W. E. Parks, exrs. 7 Feb. 1834.
Signed: W. L. Arick. Wit: A. A. Halsey, Thos. H. Hamilton, John B. Cherry.

p. 8. Will of John Hamilton, of Holmes County, Miss., 12 July 1834. To wife, Sarah,
my five negroes (named), cattle, horses, Household furniture, etc. She is to support
my children from proceeds of dowry until my youngest child, Joel, is of age.
Children: Lucinda, Clarissa, Margaret Mary, Mary Ann, Eliza Armada, son Joel and
Martha Willis. Signed: John Hamilton and James M. James,
exrs. Wit: Wm. Overstreet, Beverly Russell, W. W. Gordon.

p. 9. John L. Noble's will, 26 May 1835. To my two sisters, Mary Baskins and Sarah
Baskins, 100 acres adj. Ezekiel Calhoun, Esq., to nephew James Noble, rest of my
estate. To sister, Mary Baskins, a negro named Bill, not liable to debts of her
husband, Thos. S. Baskins; to sister Sarah Baskins, negro Jim and woman Lizzy, upon
her paying her sister, Mary, $200; something for the support of my sister-in-law,
Betsy Noble. My friends, John Baskin and Patrick Calhoun exrs. Signed. Witness:
P. Calhoun, Jas. Hutton, Patrick Noble. Abbeville Dist., S. C. Ordinance Office.
I do hereby certify that the foregoing is a true copy from the records of the office,
given under my hand and seal, 1 Apr. 1837. Signed: Moses Poggart, A. D.

p. 10. Will of Wm. G. Gary, Aug. 1, 1834. To wife, Anne, choice of three horses, etc.,
and one-third of the negroes exclusive of Judy and Lucy; sister, Mary Cocke and her
three children, Thomas M., Susan and Minerva, to have $300 per annum for five years.
My beloved wife and children, my exrs, to sell land and buy home for my children
in my own immediate neighborhood where I am about to move in Carroll County.
My good friend, Joseph Morris, sole exr. Signed Wm. G. Gary. Wit: Jas. G. Hall, Wm.
M. Brown.

p. 10. John J. (or I) Mastin's Will, of Holmes Co., Miss., Sept. 8, 1834. Estate to my
three sisters, Elizabeth, Rebecca and Mary Ann Jane. Signed with a mark. Wit:
Francis Powell, James G. Hall, Peter Powell, Wesley M. Cabenth.

p. 11. Creighton Ward's Will, Nov. 3, 1832. Wife, Nancy, sons, James, William and
Jefferson. Wife to keep property together until son James os of age. Wit: Wm. Nall, Sr.
Reuben Watts, Wm. C. Nall. Ack. in court by Wm. Nall, Sr., and Reuben Watts. (n. d.)

Will of John Lipford, Holmes Co., Miss. Legatees: my sister, Nancy Lipford, of
Virginia, a negro girl, as well as an equal share of all my estate with all my sisters
and brothers, except the part hereafter named. Negro girl, Luza, to my sister, Elizabeth,
in Virginia and a share of my estate, my brother, Thomas Lipford, of Va., an equal
share and two negro girles; to my sister, Peace, one equal share; to my brother,
Amos Lipford, of Va. and my sister, Jane Giles, equal shares, after two negroes
are given my sisters above-named. Brothers, Amos and Thomas, executors and to
act for sisters, Nancy and Elizabeth. 18 Nov. 1834. John (x) Lipford. Wit: Sam'l.
Atcherson, Wm. Purdom.

p. 11. Will of Isaac Jackson, of Madison Co., Ala., Dec. 8, 1837. To my daughter,
Nancy Auld, land (described) and one-half of Connelly grant (described); to
son, Samuel S. Jackson, two quarters, known as Banfield's; to Nancy Auld one-
third of personal estate; to son, Samuel, one-third of personal estate; to . . . .
(nothing more recorded, probably burned

Book 1.

p.13. Will of Stephem Mathews, of Holmes Co., Miss. May 3, 1838. To wife, Rebecca, slaves (listed); after her death they go to my two sons, Stephen G. Mathews and Reuben Mathews, also all money due me in Alabama; to son Archibald slaves (listed), also my landed estate in Henry Co., Alabama, on which son Archibald now resides, and after his death to Sarah Jane Mathews and Stephen Mathews, children of sd Archibald B. Mathews and Charlotte, his wife, and all his children which may be born to him in lawful wedlock; $7280 owed me by my son Reuben to be divided between him and my son Stephen G. Mathews. To son, Reuben, one-half interest in land on which I now live in Holmes County. Wit': Everet E. Ford, Hilliard H. Fatheree.

p.24. Mch. 6, 1830. State of Miss. Yazoo County. Will of James Bains. To beloved wife, Katherine, for widowhood or natural life. As soon as debts are paid, a negro girl, aged 6 to 10, shall be bought for Lavenia Ann Jefferson Wyatt; as soon as son, George Simmons Bains, comes of age, one-fifth of my estate to be given him, allowing enough for education , etc., of my younger children; as soon as my son, James Spivey Bains comes of age, one-fourth of estate to him, allowing enough for education for my youngest child; when my son, Samuel Cornelius Bains comes of age, one third of estate to him. If wife marries or dies, balance to be divided equally among my three sons. Signed: James Bains. Wit: John M. McMorrow, Burwell Scott, Wm. McCormack.

p.56. April 15, 1845. Will of William Eggleston. Beloved wife, Fanny P. Eggleston: Children. Proved by Richard T. Archer, Thos. Giles.

p.65. Will of Wm. Hampton, Holmes Co., Miss. June 6, 1845. To beloved wife, S. W. Hampton all real, personable and perishable estate during natural life to raise minor children; after her death to be divided amongst my legal heirs as follows: Have given Martha K. Urbey negro man, value to be taken from her part of my estate. Divide equally. Son Herbert T. Hampton and Wm. Anderson, exrs. Signed: Wm. Hampton. Attest: A. Lemon, S. D. Anderson. Prob. Sept. Term 1845 by Anderson.

p.76. Will of Dorothy C. Jones, Aug. 28, 1847. Legatees: Father, Peter Jones, Nora and Samuel Jones, children of my brother, Daniel Jones; brother Thomas Jones, Thos. G. Clark, exr. Wit: G. H. Worthington. Prob. Dec. 6, 1847.

p.108. 28 June 1849. Will of Wm. H. Wade, of Holmes Co. Sister Lucinda Thurmond, books, desk and note against P. B. Thurmond, Oct. 13, 1847, for $2040, and her daughters, Susan A. E., Martha L., and Mary L. Thurmond. To my daughter, Georgeanna S. Wade, two-thirds of my property, real and personal, to embrace slaves possessed by me in right of her mother, Susan E. Wade. To my son, James B. Wade, the remaining one-third including slaves given me by his grandfather, Manoah Bolton, not from any want of love and affection for son but for reason that he will be amply provided for by his grandfather, Stephen B. Walton and Wm. C. Saffold, exrs. In case of death of either, James N. McLean, or both James M. Wilson, substitute exrs. Signed Wm. H. Wade. Wit: W. H. Legrand, W. B. Smart, Robt. H. Pullin.

p.110. Alfred M. Jones' Will, Jany. 23, 1852. Sons, Hamilton and John S. Jones; wife, Sealy S. Jones; two sisters, Biddy Teague, wife of John R. Teague, and Margaret Weatherford, wife of Elihu Weatherford. Brother, Clinton Jones, exr. Signed Alfred M. Jones. Prob. Feb. 3, 1852.

p.132. Will of Hezekiah Harrington, Mch. 31, 1852. Weak in body. Legatees: Heirs of son, John B. Harrington, dec'd., daughter Mary J. Thomas, wife of D. C. Thomas; son Kennedy Harrington, $2500; son Edward Harrington, $2000, son Wm. C. Harrington $2000; son Ivy Harrington $4000; Fletcher Harrington $2000. (continued next page)

Book 1.

p. 132. (cont.) son, Whitfield Harrington, $2100; Ann E. Murphy $2300; Laura L.
Harrington 7 slaves (value $3000), a horse and saddle ($125) and bed and furniture
($50); grandson Edward H. Harrington $800.   dividing slaves no separating of man
and wife and as little scattering of families as possible. Kennedy Harrington and
Fletcher Harrington, exrs. Signed. Wit: Jno. P. Coleman, John Gray, George M. Weatherby. Prob. June 6, 1853.

p. 137. Will of James H. Herbert, weak. Estate to dear wife and child. My wife's
property to remain in her own hands. James H. Douglass, Robert Craig and Geo. M.
Weatherby, exrs. Nov. 10, 1853. Will made and dated Oct. 7, 1853, sworn to by
Douglass.

p. 152. Will of Thomas Wright, once of Essex Co., Va., now of Holmes Co., Miss.
Estate, except specified bequest to be kept together, money in good hands, negroes
hired and place rented out for four years after my death until my son, Kirkham
Brantley Wright arrives at 21 years. Purpose to provide for his maintenance and
education at the best schools. But should my mother die before he reaches such
age, I give my son, K. B. Wright, all my patrimonial estate, including land and
negroes. Should the amount thus falling to him at my mother's death not be worth
$8000 then I will the deficiency be made up out of any part of my estate either
in Miss. or elsewhere. The farm, above-mentioned, at the end of four years, I will
to the children of my son, Selden Wright, to be taken in his hands, as their trustee,
also a servant man, Joe and his son, Ben, to S. S. Wright as trustee for his children,
also the amount of his indebtedness to me at the time of my death, provided it
is not more than $1500. If over, the excess to be part of my estate. I wish Selden
Wright as trustee, also to receive for his children $100 as a remuneration to him
for a set of drawers which I gave his aunt Roan, when he was a child, and for which
I have grieved. Should either child die without issue, I will that the surviving
inherit jointly; should all his children die without issue, I will that none but my
own grandchildren inherit. My son, Selden S. Wright to give no security as trustee
for his children.   Having done so much more for Thomas during my life than his
dear mother requested, for which I fear he was the least thankful of all, should
his children live to the age of 25 years, I wish all the negroes I acquired by marriage with his mother to be equally divided equally between them, this division
to take place upon the 1st child arriving at that age, and those of tender age, I
wish theirs to be placed in the hands of trustee for their benefit and to have their
portions of the negroes assigned them as each arrives at that age. The negroes to
be hired out, year after year, but I do not wish my son, Thomas, or his wife, to
hire any. Should there be an accumulation of funds from the hire of my negroes
and other sources, after doing as directed to and by my son, Kirkham Brantley
Wright, I wish it every year set apart in good hands and every two years divided,
as follows: to S. S. Wright, as trustee of his children one-third; to the children
of my son, Thomas, one-third, (to be paid into good hands), and to the children
of my daughter Emily, one-third, to be placed in the hands of her husband as
trustee, until my son, K. B. Wright is twenty-one or gets his patrimonial
estate (that is, my father's and mother's estate.) I now direct that the negroes
and their increase I may leave, which I acquired by marriage with the mother of
my daughter, Emily, be taken possession of by John P. Povall, only as trustee for
my daughter Emily, also my household and kitchen furniture, except my mahogany
bookcase to her daughter, Ann G. Wright, a mahogany table(small) to my grand-
daughter, Mary Shepherd Wright. Should my daughter Emily die without (other) issue
then I, wish her surviving child to inherit all I give her. Mr. Povall's indebtedness to me, by bond, of $1000, which I leave in the hands of trustee for my dau.
Emily, to be applied to her benefit when Kirkham is 21, or gets the estate I leave
him. $500 of the balance of his indebtedness I leave to S. S. Wright, trustee for
his children. This I give him to make up the amount the Tan Yard was worth.
The balance of Povall's debt to be equally divided between the children of(con't)

Book 1.

p. 162, (cont.) my son, Tom S.S. Wright, for his children and the child or children
of my daughter, Emily. Signed Thos. Wright. (n.d.) // To my four granddaughters,
Mary Stuart Wright, Mary Shepherd Wright, Nanie Brooks Wright and Ann G.W.
Povall, I give my land, or lots on Tuckahoe Hill in Lexington. Should either of
these four die, the survivor or survivors to inherit. If Mary Shepherd should inherit,
the place to be in the hands of John Povall, for her benefit. 11 July 1855. Son, S.S.
Wright and John Povall, exrs. Signed Thos. Wright. Codocil. To my dear children,
Selden, Emily and son-in-law John Povall, I commit my dearest little tender,
motherless, dependant and necessetous infant, Kirkham Brantly Wright, may the
blessing of heaven attend him. Thos. Wright. //Codocil. As my son Thomas's children
do not get their negroes until they are 25 years of age, whereas the others get their
portions when my son Kirkham is 21, I will that the profits of the negroes willed
to the children of my son Thomas from that time be set aside yearly but not distributed. July 25, 1855. Thos. Wright. // Codocil. I have provided herein that the
children of my son Thomas, except Mary Shepherd, should not directly receive
benefits of my estate until they arrive at the age of 25 years, it is my will that
they share equally the same upon arriving at the years of 21, as all other children's
children. Feb. 14, 1856. Thos. Wright. Wit: Benj. W. Morton. Probate Feb. 1858.
Appeared A. G. Otey, Thos. S. Wright, Abram Schild. Will, July 11, 1855.

p. 175. April 23, 1847. Mahulda Land's Will. Property to be kept together until my
youngest child arrives at the age of 18 or marries. Andrew J. McDonald, exr. Wit:
Jason L. Jordan, John F. Hobbs, Wm. Smith Chew. Prob. Aug. 24, 1857.

p. 189, Will of James Olive. May 15, 1853. My estate to my daughter Ailsey, as
intended by her mother, my late wife, as the children of my wife, by her former
husband, have been amply provided for. Wit: B. T. Owen, W. Brooke. May 17, 1858.

p. 195. Will of Caroline C. Johnson. Dec. 14, 1848. Have given Silas and Joshua
McBee 20 negroes apiece. The property to be divided between the four younger
children. There may not be quite as much as the older children have gotten.
Charles, Joseph and Isaac to live in home place with Margaret. Joshua McBee
executor. Wit: John McCampbell, Margaret Harbour, 3. W. Treadwell. Prob. Jan. 17,
1859.

p. 208. Will of Clinton Jones, May 2, 1859. Son, Clinton H. Jones, $30,000; daughter
Mary Ann Tate, wife of Waddy Tate, $19,125 (making $35,000); Thomas Tabb Jones;
dau. Harriet Amanda Jones; dau. Sarah Katherine Jones. Wit: Elias Taylor, Peter A.
Parker, O. C. Taylor. Prob. Sept. 19, 1859.

p. 205. Will of Susan J. Farr, Holmes Co., Miss. 6 Mch. 1859. Being about to depart
this life, to my son, James E. Farr, farm of 160 acres I now live on and negro Eliza.
To Sarah E. Hosea, negro girl Mariah, her increase to be equally divided among my
children, B. R. Farr, J. J. Farr, Patrick H. Farr and Sarah A. Hosea. Negro man Sam and
and my perishable property equally divided between my childre, leaving out my
daughter, Sarah A. Hosea, and giving my son, Geo. W. Farr, $200 the advantage in
the division. My daughter, E. A. Clower, shall not be charged in the division with
the sum of $110 held against her in the Probate Ct. of this county. Son, James E.
Farr, executor. Signed: Susan J. Farr. Wit: Samuel Buffkin, M. N. Tidwell. Prob. Apr.
Term 1859.

p. 209. Will of Jesse B. Walton, June 4, 1859. Sick. Nuncupative will. To wife,
America J. Walton, my cook Ann and her husband, John, more than her share of my
estate. Son, James M. Walton, over his share of my estate. Wit: David Sutton, J. M.
McLean, G. A. McLean, John T. Walton. Prob. Sept. 19, 1856.

Book 1.

p. 253. Will of Sarah Wade. Aug. 13, 1856. Whereas my two sons, Henderson S. and William H. Wade, (now dec'd.), having been more fortunate in pecuniary respects and their children more comfortably provided for than the children of my only daughter, Lucinda, wife of James P. Thurmond, now, while cherishing equal natural affection for all my grandchildren, I give all my property, as follows: To James P. Thurmond and Henderson W. Thurmond, as trustee for the use and benefit of Wm. T., Georgiana and Edw. W. Wade, children of said Henderson S. Wade, by his last marriage, $1000. To grandson of daughter, Lucinda and Pow-hatan Thurmond, a negro. To grandchildren, Susan E. Walton, Martha L. and Mary L. Thurmond, ... To grandson, James P. Thurmond, son of daughter, Lucinda and Powhatan Thurmond, negro. To dau., Lucinda and her husband land for granddaughters. Negroes to children of my grandson, Fielding L. Thurmond, to wit: Stephen Horton, John T. David, Wylie T. Lane. Prob. Feb. 25, 1861.

p. 262. Nuncupative will of James Walton. Jan. 18, 1861. Wife to remain on place and things to remain as they are till her death. Son, James F. Walton to attend to business. Witnesses: Mary H. Sample, Josephine S. Harrington, Ivy F. Harrington, James H. Douglas, July 22, 1861.

p. 287. William Clower's Will. Holmes Co., Dec. 1860. To my beloved wife, land I reside on (descp), during her natural life, also slaves, to be under the control and management of Powell Harvey and my son, Benj. R. Clower, for the support of my wife, and what is left to be paid annually to my three sons, John, Benj. R. and Green R. Clower. At her death, all to three sons and grandchildren: Thomas, Manson, Daniel, Pettus and Pinckney Lehr and their sister Lavinia Cole, wife of Thos. H. Cole, $500 each, to grandchildren, Wm. Webster and Jackson Millsaps $25 each; to gr. ch. Lavinia and Eliza Millsaps and to Mrs. Rebecca Bowen and grandson, Franklin Millsaps $800. Signed: William Clower. Wit: G. W. Farr, Jno. W. Bailey, W. L. Stark. Prob. Jany. 27, 1862.

p. 288. Will of John M. West. Mch. 10, 1843. To beloved wife, Ailsey S. West, whole estate. Exr. B. T. Owen. Wit: N. W. Hoskins, J. M. Dyer, W. W. Walton. Prob. Dec. 30, 1843.

p. 291. Will of William E. Cunliffe. May 27, 1861. To mother, Ann H. Cunliffe, all personal property and real estate in Holmes County, Miss., also in Chesterfield Co., Va., and at her death to my brother, J. R. Cunliffe. Stephen Eggleston, executor. Wit: W. A. Drennan. Probated Jan. 26, 1864.

pp. 313-5. Will of Frances C. Meade. Son, Thomas Tabb Meade and Thos. Tabb Bolling executors. Daughters: Fanny T. Meade, Rebecca Bolling Meade, Mary Everard Meade; son David Kidder Meade; gr-daughter Frances Bolling Meade, dau. of Thos. T. Meade. Wit: John C, Ramsey, Mary P. Ramsey. Dec. 14, 1852. // Codocil, June 22, 1857. To daughter, Elizabeth Randolph Grant, wife of Prior W. Grant, and Seignora Peyton Smith, wife of George N. Smith; my deceased husband's nephew, John Peyton Eggleston. Wit: Stephen Eggleston, Seignora B. Jones, Henry K. Jones. (No date of probate.)

p. 316. Will of James M. Segar. To Selden Wright, son of my relative, Thomas S. Wright, my silver watch; to Selden Wright and Sue Lina Wright, children of Thos. S. Wright. Thos. W. Wright executor. Aug. 3, 1861. Signed: James M. Segar. Wit: J. P. Povall, Wm. Boyle. Prov. May 28, 1866.

p. 322. Will of Mrs. A. S. West. Ailsey S. West, being feeble and feeling a deep anxirty for the maintenance and education of my younger children, etc. Children: Jess T., Sarah A., Joseph B., Mary E., Olive, and Salina H. West, house and lot in Lexington. William A. West, son, exr. Oct. 1, 1866. Wit: Benj. Griffin, J. M. Haynes, M. D. Haynes.

Book 1.

p. 327-8. Will of Mary Jane Wilson. Legatee: Daughter, Maria L. Perry. Jan. 23, 1867. Probated October 28, 1868.

p. 324. Will of Israel Pickens, Sept. 12, 1867. Son, Joseph W. D. Pickens; wife, Mary R.; son, Israel B. Pickens; daughters, Martha J. Pickens, Louisa B. Pickens. Wit: John Falls, J. W. Wade, James I. Pickens. Probated February 24, 1868.

p. 340. Will of George W. Stigler. Apr. 14, 1869. To each of the children $100; grandchildren, Narcissa Williams and Mary Clower, children of Benjamin R. Clower, $100; wife, Catherine Stigler. Son, Isaac R. Stigler, executor. Wit: C. H. Weston, A. B. Green, J. J. Hooker. Probated Sept. 9, 1870.

p. 371. Will of Martha E. Stigler, May 10, 1873. Husband, Ed B. Stigler. Daughter, Bettie E. Rogers; William P. Rogers; son Stephen E. Stigler, none of age. Eldest daughter, Susan Ella Gilliam. My father, William Anderson. Wit: W. H. M. Durham, H. D. Gray, Jr., Thos. R. Owen. Probated September 13, 1873.

p. 876. Will of William Stigler. 15 April 1873. Wife and my daughter, by her, Mary Hamilton, one-half each of my two-thirds interest in lands on which I now reside, to be undivided until my said daughter comes of age or marries. Balance of estate to my beloved wife, my son, Simeon, and daughter, Mary Hamilton, to be divided equally. Brother, James M. Stigler, executor and guardian of son, Simeon. Wit: George E. Young, John K. Harring, M. Levy. Probated November 25, 1873.

p. 480. Will of James M. Wilson, December 18, 1884. Wife, Emmeline M. Wilson, all my worldly estate. At her death, same to be divided between children and grandchild, Bettie Wilson. Probated December 1st, 1885.

HARRISON COUNTY, GULFPORT

Deeds.

Bk. 13-376. Sarah A. Dorsey from A. F. Johnston.

July 7, 1873. Frank Johnstone, of Jackson, Miss., sells to Sarah A. Dorsey, wife of Samuel W. Dorsey, for $3500 cash, the following lands, (six, aggregating 882 acres, location given). Also a lot at West Biloxi, fronting the Sea Shore, No. 14, one and one-half arpents front by 8 arpents deep. All said lands in Harrison County, being lands owned by James Brown at the time of his death and known as the Brown Place, sold under decree of the U. S. Court, Southern District of Mississippi and conveyed by James Stewart and Archie McGehee, special commissioners, May 1873, to grantor. Signed Frank Johnston. Ack. July 7, 1873.

Bk. 16-328. Indenture between Sarah A. Dorsey and Jefferson Davis, both of Harrison Co., Miss., 19 Feb. 1879. Sarah A. Dorsey, of Harrison Co., Miss., to Jefferson Davis; for $5500, to be paid as follows, $1000 Jany. 1st, 1880; $2000 Jany. 1st, 1881; $2500 Jany. 1st, 1882; for which Jefferson Davis has given me promisory notes; tracts and parcels of land in said county (described as in preceding deed.) Also all the household and kitchen furniture and all the personal property now in dwelling house on lot on the beach at West Biloxi and on said lands, except the pictures, engravings, books, silver plate and ware, piano, harp and all the articles of virtue, and an old horse known as Rupert. Signed: Sarah Ann Dorsey. Ack. Feb. 19, 1879.

Deed Bk. 16-361.

March 20, 1879. Sarah A. Dorsey, Vendor, and Jefferson Davis, Vendee, all of Harrison Co., the following conditions annexed to and become a part of a certain deed of conveyance of real estate and personal property, (as recorded above) To wit: I. In the contingency of the death of the Vendee, Jefferson Davis, before the payment of the notes recited in the said deed, the same shall them become null and void and the said real and personal estate shall revert to Vendor, Sarah A. Dorsey, refunding to the Vendee any payments which he may have made on the said notes. II. If vendee should at any time before the payment of the notes afsd. desire to restore said real and personal estate he shall have the right to do so and be relieved from the payments of the notes. III. In event of the re-delivery of the said real and personal estate to the Vendor then the Vendee, Jefferson Davis, shall in his natural life retain the joint interest in the vineyard as it existed before the contract of sale. IV. If neither of the above-named contingencies arise and all the notes be paid the Vendor, Sarah A. Dorsey, shall never-the-less retain and hold, during her natural life an equal interest in the vineyard and orange grove of Beauvoir which shall be cultivated and gathered in joint account. V. If the contract shall be rescinded all personal property shall be delivered to the afsd. Vendor, for which an inventory of the same shall be delivered to afsd Vendor, for which an inventory of the same shall be made in duplicate. Signed Sarah Ann Dorsey, Jefferson Davis. Ack. 11, 1879.

Will Book 2, p. 212. Last will and Testament of Mrs. Sarah Ann Dorsey, from the copy thereof in Will Book 20, of the late 2nd District Court, folios 160-162. Mrs. Sarah Ann Dorsey, Ne Variture, N. O., July 15, 1879.   Jan. 4th, 1878. Beauvoir, Harrison Co,, Miss. I, Sarah Ann Dorsey, of Tensas Parish, Louisiana, being aware of the uncertainty of life and being now in sound health of mind and body, do make this my last will and testament, which I write and sign with my own hand in the presence of three competent witnesses as I possess property in the States of Louisiana, Mississippi and Arkansas. I owe no obligation of any sort whatever to any relative of my own. I have done all I could for them during my life. I, therefore, give and bequeath all my property, real, personal and mixed, where located and situated, wholly and entirely, without hindrance or qualification, to my most honored and esteemed friend, Jefferson Davis, Ex-President of the Confederate States, for his sole use and benefit in fee simple forever and I hereby constitute him my sole heir, executor and administrator. If Jefferson Davis should not survive me I give all that I have bequeathed him to his youngest daughter, Varina. I do not intend to share in the ingratitude of my country towards the man who is, in my eyes, the highest and noblest in existence. In testimony whereof I sign this will written in my own hand in presence of W. T. Walthall, F. S. Hewes and John S. Craig, subscribing witnesses, resident in Harrison County, Miss. Signed: Sarah Ann Dorsey. At Mississippi City on Jan. 4, 1878, above acknowledged same. This case, No. 1342, Civil District Court, No. 41, 376. // Succession of Mrs. S. A. Dorsey, No. 1342, Civil District Court, Division D. Order: Let the last will and testament of the deceased be proved before me forthwith. Signed: A. T. Tissot, Judge. N. O. July 15, 1879.

Alston, Philip	10,19	Cook, Tyree	13	Green, Evd.	10
Anderson, Sarah	15	William	13	Elizabeth	13
Armstrong, John	9	Cowdon, J.	12	Jane	11
Richard	13	Jas., Jr.	12	Henry	11
Sarah	13	Cox, Henry H.	9	Thos. M.	11
Atkinson, John	18	Craig, Eliza	16	Greenleaf, Dan'l.	14
Brazeale, D. W.	11	Fenton N.	16	Griffing, W.	14
Bartholomew, Elizabeth	14	Henry	13,14,16	Harris, Levi C.	9,12,16
Willis	14	Phebe	14,16	Roxana	10
Bay Elihu Hall	11	Rachel	16	Hartley, Mrs. Deborah	14
Bedsel, James	18	William H.	16	Harriet	14
Berthe, Charlotte M.	19	Curtis, Wm.	9	Mary Ann	14
James	19	Davidson, Marie	15	John	14
Blanton, Edmund	19	John A.	10	Hill, Caleb	18
John	18,19	Sidney	19	Hinds, Edward	10
Sarah	18,19	David, David	17	Thos.	9,12,15
W. W.	19	Dennie, John	18	Hogan, Rauleigh	17
Brandt, John	10	Dillingham, Vachel, Jr.	14	Hopkins, John	10
Brooks, Celeste	11	Dixon, Roger	9	Hospinsed	10
George	16	Dobbs, John	13,16	Hunt, Abijah	10,11
John	9	John H.	13	D.	12
S.	12	Doherty, Jno	11	David	12
William	9,10,12	Downs, Henry D.	10	Humphreys, G. W.	9,15
Bruin, Bryan	10	Dow Joseph	10	Geo. Wilson	9
Bullen, Benj. M.	14	Joshua	11,15	Hunter, Milford	14
Burney, John	18	Droomgoolw, Jas.	19	James, Daniel	9,12
Richard D.	18	Dunbar, Jo	12	Jeffers, Sally P.	15
Callaghan, Daniel	19,10	Joseph	18	Johnson A.	14
Calvit, Thomas	11	Elliott, James	10	John C.	10,
Camberlain, James	10	Ellis James, Jr.	10	Jas.	14
Campbell, James	9	Ellis, Armstrong	17	Jones, Elizabeth	14,15
Carradine, Parker	12	Ferguson, Nathan	10	Jonathan	14
Chambers, Daniel	9	William	12	John	14
Chambliss, Peter	12	Fitzpatrick, Thos.	12,19	Zachariah	14
Claiborne, Ferdinand	9	Flanarty, Ferdinand	9	Jouet, Everet H.	14
Clack, James	16	Fletcher, Margaret	13	Jourdan, Chas. H	16
Clare, George	11	Samuel	13	Kempe, James	9
Cloud, Adam	15	Foster, Ann	13	Ker, Martha	15
Cole, Mary	12	Helen Jane	,16	King, David	15
Susannah	15	James David	9,16	Prosper	15
Coleman, Blackman	13	John	9,16	Kirkland, Zachariah	9
Elizabeth	14	Martha	9,16	Leake, Walter	9
Israel	14	Mary	16	Lee, Charles L.	19
Pharoby	13	Mary Eliza	16	Lenard, Eunice	14
Collier, Mary	11	Moses	14	Lewis, Seth	11
William	11,15	William	12	Liddell, Moses	11
Cook, Elizabeth	16	Fulgham, John S.	16	Lovell, Mariah	12
Fielding	13	Gibson, David	12	Thomas	12
Jane	13	Randall	12,15	Lum, Jesse	12
Jesse	13,14,16,18	Girault, Francis	9	Hannah	12
Rachael	13,16,18	Jno.	9,18	William	12

INDEX, HINDS COUNTY

www.ingramcontent.com/pod-product-compliance
Lightning Source LLC
Chambersburg PA
CBHW072208270326
41930CB00011B/2577